Becoming the People of God

Walking Humbly, Doing Justice

By J. Richard Peck

Cokesbury / Nashville

Becoming the People of God:
Walking Humbly, Doing Justice

Copyright © 2002 by Cokesbury

This book is printed on recycled, acid-free paper.

ISBN 0-687-51193-7

03 04 05 06 07 08 09 10 11—10 9 8 7 6 5 4 3 2

*Walking Humbly,
Doing Justice*

Table of Contents

Introduction

Methodists have a long history of concern for social justice. Its members have often taken forthright positions on controversial issues involving Christian principles. Early Methodists expressed their opposition to the slave trade, to smuggling, and to the cruel treatment of prisoners.

The Methodist Episcopal Church (North) adopted a social creed in 1908. Within the next decade, The Methodist Episcopal Church, South, and The Methodist Protestant Church adopted similar statements.

The Evangelical United Brethren Church adopted a statement of Social Principles in 1946 at the time of the uniting of The United Brethren and The Evangelical Church.

In 1972, four years after the uniting in 1968 of The Methodist Church and The Evangelical United Brethren Church, the General Conference of the United Methodist Church adopted a new statement of Social Principles. (See *The Book of Resolutions of The United Methodist Church, 2000;* pages 37–64.) Meeting every four years since that time, the General Conference of the united denomination has revised those principles.

Most of the Social Principles and resolutions are the result of individuals, local churches, or agencies writing petitions to be considered by the nearly 1,000 delegates to General Conference. These petitions are considered in legislative committees that recommend acceptance, rejection, or amendments. All delegates then vote on these recommendations.

The Preface to the Social Principles says they are "intended to be instructive and persuasive in the best of the prophetic spirit." They are a call to 9.4 million members of The United Methodist Church "to a prayerful, studied dialogue of faith and practice." There is no need for readers to agree with every statement, and this book will offer suggestions for classes to address differences in opinion.

This book is based on the Social Community section of the Social Principles statement as adopted by the 2000 General Conference held in Cleveland, Ohio (¶162). Chapters include resolutions related to the topics as well as suggestions for individual actions, reports on actions taken by local churches, and teaching plans for small groups.

It is unlikely that a study group will be able to use all the suggested activities in a single session, and leaders will probably want to continue the study of a chapter over several weeks. However, we hope that this study will not end with this book but will lead to appeals for legislation; actions in local communities; and efforts to build loving relationships with children, aging adults, persons suffering from addictions, and persons of different genders, races, cultures, and faith communities.

After you complete this study, you may want to seek others in the six-volume *Becoming the People of God* series. Locate them at *cokesbury.com*, at your local Cokesbury store, or by calling Curric-U-Phone (800-251-8591).

Preface to
The Social Community
Section of the Social Principles

SOCIAL PRINCIPLE ¶162

*T**he rights and privileges a society bestows upon or withholds from those who constitute it indicate the relative esteem in which that society holds particular persons and groups of persons. We affirm all persons as equally valuable in the sight of God. We therefore work toward societies in which each person's value is recognized, maintained, and strengthened. We support the basic rights of all persons to equal access to housing, education, employment, medical care, legal redress for grievances, and physical protection. We deplore acts of hate or violence against groups or persons based on race, ethnicity, gender, sexual orientation, religious affiliation, or economic status.*

(*Book of Resolutions*, page 46)

Chapter 1

Rights of Racial and Ethnic Persons

Social Principle ¶162A, "Rights of Racial and Ethnic Persons"

Racism is the combination of the power to dominate by one race over other races and a value system that assumes that the dominant race is innately superior to the others. Racism includes both personal and institutional racism. Personal racism is manifested through the individual expressions, attitudes, and/or behaviors that accept the assumptions of a racist value system and that maintain the benefits of this system. Institutional racism is the established social pattern that supports implicitly or explicitly the racist value system. Racism plagues and cripples our growth in Christ, inasmuch as it is antithetical to the gospel itself. White people are unfairly granted privileges and benefits that are denied to persons of color. Therefore, we recognize racism as sin and affirm the ultimate and temporal worth of all persons. We rejoice in the gifts that particular ethnic histories and cultures bring to our total life. We commend and encourage the self-awareness of all racial and ethnic groups and oppressed people that lead them to demand their just and equal rights as members of society. We assert the obligation of society and groups within the society to implement compensatory programs that redress long-standing, systemic social deprivation of racial and ethnic people. We further assert the right of members of racial and ethnic groups to equal opportunities in employment and promotion; to education and training of the highest quality; to nondiscrimination in voting, in access to public accommodations, and in housing purchase or rental; to credit, financial loans, venture capital, and insurance policies; and to positions of leadership and power in all elements of our life together. We support affirmative action as one method of addressing the inequalities and discriminatory practices within our Church and society.

Core Bible Passages

Matthew 5:38-48; 2 Corinthians 4, 5:16-21; Acts 10:34; Ephesians 2:8-22

Three years ago, *Newsweek* magazine carried an article entitled "The Good News About Black America (and Why Many Blacks Aren't Celebrating)." The article included two pages of graphs showing how black Americans were moving forward in education, health, home life, and economics. The report showed there has been a steady climb in black educational achievement and health since the early 1970s.

Optimism within the African American community is growing. When asked whether they thought that their quality of life had risen in the last five years, 59 percent of blacks and 53 percent of whites said their income was better; 43 percent of blacks and 40 percent of whites thought their job opportunities were better; and 38 percent of blacks and 30 percent of whites thought their education quality was better than it was five years ago.

When looking ten years into the future, 71 percent of blacks thought their family income would rise, while only 59 percent of whites thought the same. Sixty-four percent of blacks expected to see improvements in their local schools, but only 55 percent of whites thought the same. Fifty-seven percent of blacks saw more job opportunities ahead, while only 48 percent of whites did. So blacks seemed to see things improving for themselves at a faster rate than their white counterparts.

Despite the optimism of the black population, it cannot mask the wide disparities between white and black persons in our nation. Blacks continue to have lower incomes than whites, constitute a disproportionate percentage of the poor, are more likely to be imprisoned or to be the victims of a homicide or other violent crime, and are less likely to own a home or have health insurance.

The "whites only" segregation signs that once marked water fountains and bathrooms are now a generation behind us, but racism remains an ugly wound that plagues our communities and slows true progress toward equality of opportunity.

Despite the optimism about the future, blacks interviewed in the article showed little faith that they would ever reach true economic parity with whites. When asked whether blacks would ever be able to earn as much money as whites, only 42 percent of blacks responded "yes" while 71 percent of whites did.

A Call for Reparations for African Americans

Noting that at the conclusion of the Civil War, the plan for the economic redistribution of land and resources on behalf of the former slaves of the

Confederacy was never enacted, The United Methodist Church has called for reparation payments to African Americans.

The 1996 General Conference noted that "the failure to distribute land prevented newly freed blacks from achieving true autonomy and made their civil and political rights all but meaningless." Observing that economic depression continues for millions of African Americans in communities where unemployment often exceeds 50 percent accompanied by unabated narcotics trafficking and gang killings, the denomination says these realities can be traced to the broken promise that each slave would receive "forty acres, fifty dollars, and a mule."

The denomination is calling for a discussion and study of reparations for African Americans and is asking the United States House of Representatives to pass a 1993 bill submitted by Congressman John Conyers, Jr. (D-Michigan) calling for the establishment of the Commission to Study Reparation Proposals for African Americans, "acknowledging the fundamental injustice, cruelty, brutality and inhumanity of slavery in the United States from 1619 to the present day," for the purpose of submitting a report to Congress for further action and consideration with respect to slavery's effects on African American lives, economics, and politics.

Wide Support for Race-Based Arrests

Racial profiling was once a great concern of many Americans; but since the September 11, 2001, attack upon America, it has been tolerated and sometimes encouraged.

Michael Conlon of Reuters News Service tells the story of Osama El Far, an aircraft mechanic from Alexandria, Egypt.

"The police came to my job," said El Far. "They got a call from a co-worker who said I was a Muslim with access to the airport. They tell me somebody in Washington is still interested in me. They won't tell me who." El Far is now one of hundreds of Arabs and other foreigners detained in US.

A late 2001 Gallup poll found that more than one in four Americans thought President Bush and Attorney General John Ashcroft had not gone far enough in restricting civil liberties to fight terrorism. Another 60 percent of the 1,025 polled thought the actions taken so far had been "about right." A recent poll by Zogby International found that more US blacks than whites—75 percent compared to 64 percent—even supported having their car searched at random as an anti-terrorism measure, exactly the kind of "stop-first, question-later" action that had previously been so reviled in the black community.

El Far was held because he was in the country illegally on an expired student visa. The colleague who informed on him also alleged that El Far had praised Osama bin Laden, the man accused of masterminding the September 11 attacks that killed about 3,900 people. El Far denies the accusation. He also likely became a suspect because he attended flight-training school in Florida in 1996–97. Some of the suicide airline hijackers had attended Florida flight schools though much more recently.

El Far said the FBI had assured him he had been cleared, but he remains in detention. His frustration was that his case was in limbo even though he had booked a flight and was ready to leave the country.

Meanwhile, there seems to be little sympathy for persons like El Far.

Not Since World War II

The arrests that have put nearly 600 people in jail and the plans to question hundreds of other people are on a scale unseen since the start of World War II when 100,000 Japanese immigrants and Japanese Americans were interned at interior locations far from strategic coastal areas. Although public opinion polls may not show it, some people are disturbed by the parallels.

"The profiling of people from the Middle East is just a carryover of an inbred inability to see people other than ourselves as being OK," said 81-year-old Marian Spencer, a former Cincinnati city councilwoman and longtime civil rights leader in that city's black community. "If they don't act and look like us, then there must be something wrong with them. Those people who are being detained by the government should be let go as quickly as possible once the authorities have determined they have no connection with terrorism," she said. "We should have learned our lesson about how to treat foreigners in our midst from the way Japanese-born people were interned and mistreated during World War II—but I'm not sure that bothers Ashcroft and the others," Spencer added.

Ako Abdul-Samad of Des Moines, founder of an inner-city program for children and imam of a Des Moines, Iowa, mosque, states: "We can't condemn a race of people because of individuals, and we can't make that race of people pay for those individuals. It's a total violation of civil liberties and human rights."

Edwin Yohnka, communications director for the American Civil Liberties Union of Illinois, says he has seen no weakening of opposition to the racial profiling issue among blacks but believes it is too early to say if the same political will to confront the problem that existed before the September attacks will be present down the road. In New Jersey, where racial profiling hit a flashpoint with a 1998 police shooting, state Attorney General John Farmer is well aware of the way the issue has shifted.

A Redefined Issue

"Let's be blunt," he said. "How can law enforcement not consider ethnicity in investigating these crimes when that identifier is an essential characteristic of the hijackers and their supposed confederates and sponsors? Racial profiling . . . was always more complex than most cared to admit, not reducible to magic percentages or easy definition on either side. But its solution . . . has always been and remains simple: Accountability. We must establish within the police mechanisms of accountability to ensure that law enforcement's conduct is commensurate with the threats it faces."

Robert Sampson, a 50-year-old black person who lives in Bellwood near Chicago, is a meat-cutter and a Gulf War Army veteran who supports the current detentions. Asked if it would make any difference if all those detained were black, he said: "If they were suspected terrorists, I wouldn't have any problem with that."

"I look at them [the government] as doing what they have to do," he said. "If they are suspected terrorists, until they can prove different, they should be held."

Marvin Jones, a 42-year-old black truck driver from Chicago, has doubts. "It's similar to what happened to the Japanese, because they were considered guilty until proven innocent," he said. "No one cares, because there is so much hatred. These people have a right to live like anyone else, unless you have some proof. If you don't, let them go. . . . I don't think it's fair."

Native Americans Protest Indian Names as Sports Mascots

At the United Methodist 2000 General Conference, Native Americans and others protested the use of the "Chief Wahoo" mascot by the Cleveland Indians baseball team. The assembly called the caricature demeaning and urged church agencies to enter into dialogue with team owners, but no dialogue had taken place by early 2002.

Protests also have been lodged against the North Dakota University "Fighting Sioux" and other college and professional teams. At a late 2001 meeting, the Native American International Caucus (NAIC) asked the Reverend Alvin Deer, executive director of the caucus, to write a letter to Ted Brown, president of Martin Methodist College in Pulaski, Tennessee, asking that the college quit using "Indians" as a name for its athletic teams.

Protests have also surfaced over the mascot "Chief Illiniwek," who dresses in Plains Indian clothing and performs at athletic events of the University of Illinois. In 2001, the United Methodist Commission on Religion and Race gave a $10,000 grant to the Illinois Chapter of the National Coalition on Racism in Sports and Media, partly to address the mascot issue. The grant also was intended to help fund a cultural center and enable the school to work on cross-cultural issues, according to the Reverend Kenneth Deere, commission staff member.

Bishop Sharon Brown Christopher, of the Illinois Area, supported the grant, despite complaints by United Methodist alumni of the university. The Reverend Carol Lakota Eastin, a Lakota and NAIC member, told the caucus that she had applied for another grant from the General Commission on Religion and Race but was dissuaded after a conversation with Illinois Great Rivers Conference officials. The commission is considering whether she was the victim of racism. She said her conference is "like a war zone" because of the conflict.

Eastin and other members of the conference committees on Native American ministries in the Illinois Great Rivers and Northern Illinois conferences made a public statement to Illinois United Methodists in March.

"At the same time that our ministries with Native Americans are expanding, we find ourselves facing a barrier," they said. "The Illiniwek stereotype is an animated character of something called Indian by non-natives," they said. "It does not portray real native people past or present. This perpetuates the invisibility of native people who are part of almost every Illinois community."

The Native American ministries representatives said the Illiniwek figure demeans Native Americans, is a reminder of genocidal history, and ridicules a dance that is sacred to them. The real Illiniwek was an Algonquin Indian and did not dress like Plains Indians, Eastin said. In discussing why the controversy has aroused such emotions, members of the NAIC listed several factors:

- Many Americans like to think of indigenous people as dead and do not want to recognize their continued presence in society.

- The religion of many church members is merely social and has no depth.

- Many white Americans have an underlying guilt about past and present treatment of Native Americans and want to deny their guilt.

- Many white Americans do not even know the history about the treatment of Native Americans in this nation.

In a United Methodist News Service commentary about the Illiniwek controversy, Deer wrote, "In a land that is often called a Christian nation, we have Christians who defend all these mascots and even put them on a pedestal, giving them more worth than the people the mascots portray. What else can it be but idolatry when Christians say they will leave the church rather than give up their mascot [idol]?"

Deer also mentioned several positive changes as a result of the protests. He said the University of Oklahoma ceased using an Indian mascot, "Little Red," and began using a miniature Conestoga wagon representing the "Sooners," the early settlers who staked out homestead land in the state. He also said United Methodist-related Oklahoma City University changed its team name from "Chiefs" to "Stars."

Racism and the Bible

We are good at extracting pieces of Scripture and using them to support a worldview we happen to favor. A more honest approach takes into account the diverse witness of the Bible.

For example, a racist may use the "ethnic cleansing" story of Ezra 10:1-5 that calls for Judahite men to get rid of their foreign wives and children as biblical argument for racial separation. In so doing they would choose to ignore Exodus

17

22:21, which implicitly establishes solidarity between the Hebrew and the alien by reminding the Hebrews that they were once aliens.

Acts 10:34 describes Peter's expanded understanding of God as one who is not partial to a particular group. Cornelius, a Gentile, is subsequently baptized into the Christian faith, an act that obliterates ethnic boundaries as a requirement for "membership."

In Matthew 22:36-40, Jesus responded to the lawyer who asked which law is greatest by quoting from the Hebrew Scriptures calling for love of God, self, and neighbor. Again and again, the Bible portrays through its stories a growing understanding that God is merciful, just, compassionate, and inclusive. Christians are called to view all the witness of the Bible through this lens.

The richly complex insights woven through the dialogues of grace and works of "insiders" and "outsiders" and of faith and law in Ephesians 2:8-16 challenge all hostile boundaries between people. It also implicitly calls Christians to responsible acts of justice and mercy. God created everyone for "good works." In Christ, God creates a new family in which all are one. The artificial human constructs that separate us are "broken down." God's grace not only saves us through faith, it empowers us, makes us into one family through Christ, and challenges us to a life lived in harmony and peace with all the members of the family. In Christ, those who were "far off" have been "brought near." No longer "strangers and aliens," we are all members of the household of God.

Teaching Plan

1. Pray the following: "God of all people, open our hearts and minds to your presence and your love for all human beings. Help us to become more aware of the injustices of racism that persist in our culture even as we celebrate freedom. Inspire us to healing behaviors; in Christ's name we pray. Amen."

2. Roleplay. Read "Wide Support for Race-Based Arrests" (pages 13–14). Roleplay an Arab American trying to board an American Airlines airplane. Ask various participants to serve as an Arab, the operator of a metal detector, an airline official, and fellow passengers. After the roleplay, ask each participant how he or she felt about the encounter.

3. Read "A Call for Reparations for African Americans" (pages 12–13). Do you agree with the United Methodist position statement? Why? Why not? If reparations are paid, to whom should they be paid? How would you determine the amount to be given?

4. Discuss: Sunday morning has often been called "the most segregated hour in America." Discuss this label. Why do so few churches find it easy to be racially integrated in an age when people of different races work, play, and live together?

5. Discuss ways in which your church could break down the walls of separation between racial groups.

6. Read about Native American protests of Indian images for sports teams. Do these mascots affect the manner in which you view Native Americans?

Walking Humbly, Doing Justice

Local Action Reports

Wilbur Memorial United Methodist Church is located in a remote corner of the Yakama Indian Reservation in Washington State. The small congregation tutors some 70 children from kindergarten-age through fifth grade. Most of the children have learning disabilities or behavioral problems. Financial support from the US Department of Agriculture, the Yakama Nation, and private donors makes it all possible.

"I believe that education is the key to getting people where they want to go in life," said church member and teacher Glenda Hargrave. "We try to create an enthusiasm for learning here. Sometimes, the kids even ask me for homework. It's really awesome."

Teenagers benefit from the program too. High-school students are paid to work as tutors and supervisors of the children, learning valuable life skills from a job that doesn't take away too many hours from their own homework responsibilities.

Crossroads/Njia Panda United Methodist Church in Compton, California, is helping other congregations breathe new life into their worship, social outreach, evangelism, and mission. It is designated by the United Methodist Church's "Strengthening the Black Church for the 21st Century" initiative as a congregational resource center.

The Reverend Lydia J. Waters became the pastor of what was then Enterprise United Methodist Church in 1985. The Compton congregation had nearly 50 people and was located in "a community that has an unfair negative reputation across the nation," she said. The previous pastor had retired after serving 15 years of part-time ministry.

"We immediately began the journey of becoming a church that incorporated authentic protocol and worship in the tradition of the black church," said Waters. The first step was to begin the healing of internalized racism and self-hate, she said. Growth began, and by 1994, membership swelled to 350 members. The congregation was too large for its small building.

Another congregation, St. Peter's United Methodist Church, three miles away, was undergoing pains of a different kind. It had completed construction of a new sanctuary, but its membership had dwindled to 15.

20

"With prayer and planning, we relocated without losing members and merged without causing havoc," Waters said. The new church became Crossroads/Njia Panda United Methodist Church. *Njia panda* is Swahili for "crossroads."

The membership is 35 percent children, 25 percent young adults, and 30 percent middle-aged. "Our outreach has been primarily to make disciples for Jesus Christ in a community where so many others do not want to come," Waters said.

The 230-member Wentzville United Methodist Church in St. Charles County, Missouri, joined with the 285-member Faith United Church of Christ to repair the aging Grant Chapel, an African Methodist Episcopal Church. "We were just going to put up siding," says Wentzville member Gerri Bodeur. "We ended up gutting it and redoing the roof." The churches raised $18,000 for the project through barbecues and other events.

Chapter 2

Caring *for* Our Children

Social Principle ¶162C, "Rights of Children"

Once considered the property of their parents, children are now acknowledged to be full human beings in their own right, but beings to whom adults and society in general have special obligations. Thus, we support the development of school systems and innovative methods of education designed to assist every child toward complete fulfillment as an individual person of worth. All children have the right to quality education, including full sex education appropriate to their stage of development that utilizes the best educational techniques and insights. Christian parents and guardians and the Church have the responsibility to ensure that children receive sex education consistent with Christian morality, including faithfulness in marriage and abstinence in singleness. Moreover, children have the rights to food, shelter, clothing, health care, and emotional well-being as do adults, and these rights we affirm as theirs regardless of actions or inactions of their parents or guardians. In particular, children must be protected from economic, physical, emotional, and sexual exploitation and abuse.

Core Bible Passages

Matthew 18:1-5; Mark 9:33-37, 10:13-16; Luke 9:46-48, 18:15-17; 2 Timothy 1:3-7

In 2001, the United Methodist Council of Bishops renewed an initiative on Children and Poverty. Begun in 1995, the bishops noted that the crisis among children and the impoverished continues unabated and it called upon all United Methodists to "Community With Children and the Poor."

The original Initiative on Children and Poverty had three goals:

1. To reshape The United Methodist Church in response to the God who is among "the least of these" and the evaluation of everything the church is and does in the light of the impact on children and the impoverished.

2. To provide resources for understanding the crisis among children and the impoverished and enabling the church to respond.

3. To engage in evangelization: the proclamation in word and deed of the gospel of God's redeeming, reconciling, and transforming grace in Jesus Christ to and with children and those oppressed by poverty.

The Initiative began with the publication of a Foundation Document that became a stimulus for responses by annual conferences, congregations, boards and agencies, and institutions to the plight of children and the impoverished. In many ways, the Initiative is influencing the church and has had an impact on children and those who live in poverty.

While the bishops felt the first five years had been productive, they observed that much of the effort had focused on our own children and children like ours. "Too little attention had been paid to the economically poor, to the systemic causes of poverty, and to the theological and ecclesiological implications of God's identification and presence with the poor." The bishops confessed that their own lifestyles often reflect being in community with the affluent rather than in community with the poor. They sought conversion in order to live, like Jesus, in more complete community with the poor.

The council confessed that too often members had

- Treated the Initiative as an optional program or temporary missional emphasis rather than as a call to confront powerful idols and to reorder the church's priorities in accordance with the God revealed in Jesus Christ;

- Sentimentalized children and the poor and substituted acts of charity for authentic community with the impoverished;

- Appealed to a general humanitarianism rather than rooting the Initiative in the nature and the mission of God.

The Current State of Children in Poverty

The bishops compared the global economy with a "giant casino" in which the few are enormously enriched, while millions toil without prospect of a decent chance at life's necessities. Women, children, and the poor continue to be the primary victims of violence and premature death. Growing violence by children against children shockingly illustrates the poverty of spirit present in our communities and nations.

In its annual report, UNICEF points to the progress that has been made on a number of fronts with respect to the well-being of the world's children. The report notes "a number of goals remain out of reach for hundreds of millions of children throughout the world. Their lives and futures are threatened in a world marked by deeper and more intractable poverty and greater inequality between the rich and the poor, proliferating conflict and violence, the deadly spread of HIV/AIDS and the abiding issue of discrimination against women and girls. More than 1.2 billion people in the world live on less than $1 a day—more than 600 million of them children."

Moreover, HIV/AIDS killed 510,000 children under age 15 in 1998, and nearly 13 million children have been orphaned by AIDS. One hundred thirty million children do not have access to primary education.

Global economic forces, policies, and practices are creating and sustaining poverty. Transnational trade has increased to about 25 percent of the world's output of goods. A third of this trade occurs within branches of individual transnational corporations, thereby permitting many of these corporations to avoid nation-based regulation (environmental or labor laws) and the taxation that would support the welfare of national populations.

Every day about $1.5 trillion (an amount roughly equal to the size of the US federal budget for a year) moves about the globe. Only about 1 percent of this money is directly related to the purchase of goods and services. The rest is devoted to speculation in currencies, stocks, bonds, and future commodity prices generally of a very short-term nature. Because of the instability of these financial flows, developing national economies are subjected to speculative booms and busts that devastate the ability of many nations in the developing world to provide basic services to their populations.

One of the causes of impoverishment is through the accumulation of onerous debt on the part of nations least able to pay. Thus Mozambique spent twice as much in 1996 on debt service as it spent on health and education; meanwhile 25 percent of the country's children died of infectious diseases. Often these poorest countries spend more money on interest payments than they receive in loans or investments. As a result, the world's poorest nations actually subsidize the profits of the richest banks of the wealthiest nations.

The bishops note that "even when countries appear economically successful, the results can be devastating for the majority of their population. Mexico, for example, has experienced an economic growth rate of nearly 8 percent (faster than any other Latin American economy) and boasts as many billionaires as Great Britain. What is troubling is that the percentage of the population living in poverty (between 40 percent and 60 percent) actually has increased, and the purchasing power of the average wage has plummeted."

The Gap Between Rich and Poor Is Growing in the US

The disparity of wealth is not restricted to developing and least-developed economies. In the United States of America, the gap between the rich and poor has been growing to reach levels of inequality never known before. The number of poor children in the United States exceeds the number of inhabitants of the largest metropolitan area in the nation. A million and a half children have at least one parent in prison. The *Chicago Tribune* reports that "over the past 20 years, the United States has become by far the most unequal nation in the industrialized world."

The compensation gap between the average CEO and his or her worker is "closer to 500 to 1 and is growing." If the "minimum wage had grown as fast as the CEO pay in the 1990s, it wouldn't be $5.15 now but $24.13, enough to lift America's millions of working poor out of their poverty."

In the United States, nearly half of all wealth is owned by the wealthiest 1 percent, while the bottom 80 percent of the population owns only 4 percent. "In other words, the 2 million Americans at the top own 10 times as much as the 200 million further down."

This growing disparity of wealth most severely affects children. More than 25 percent of US children live in poverty, the highest rate among industrialized nations. Children of poverty are sent to the worst schools and have reduced access to health care. Mothers who live in poverty are told they must work rather than take care of their children. They are paid wages that do not get them above the poverty level. When they do find work, they often are not provided benefits or childcare.

Our economic values are contrary to the interests of children and the poor and

25

with the purposes of God revealed to us in Scripture and in Jesus Christ. The market logic, with its pervasive dependency upon consumerism, shapes modern life, including churches, and reduces everything to commodities available to those who have money to exchange. As a result, the chasm between the rich and the poor widens, and the poor are relegated to the margins of society. The chasm deepens the spiritual poverty of the prosperous and fragments Christian community. From among the poor and vulnerable people of the world, the crucified and risen Christ is calling us into a new community. It is a community formed and shaped by the God who hears the cries of the poor and incorporates them into a community formed and shaped by grace (gift) and basic life provisions for all.

Children in America

Every day in the United States:
- One person under age 25 dies from HIV infection.
- Six children and youth under 20 commit suicide.
- Ten children and youth under 20 are homicide victims.
- Ten children and youth under age 20 die from firearms.
- Thirty-four children and youth under age 20 die from accidents.
- Seventy-eight babies die.
- 156 babies are born at low birthweight (less than 52 ounces).
- 186 children are arrested for violent crimes.
- 351 children are arrested for drug abuse.
- 410 babies are born to mothers who had late or no prenatal care.
- 1,310 babies are born without health insurance.
- 1,354 babies are born to teen mothers.
- 1,951 babies are born into poverty.
- 2,324 babies are born to mothers who are not high-school graduates
- 2,911 high school students drop out.
- 4,342 children are arrested.
- 1,797 students are suspended from school.

What Can a Local Church Do?

- Create congregations in which the spiritual and material gifts of the poor and rich are shared with one another.

- Involve the indigent and the working poor in congregational life, treating them not as objects of charity but as indispensable members of the body of Christ.

- Review all aspects of the life of the church in the light of Christ's new community.

- Yoke congregations with one in a different economic bracket in order to share resources and facilities.

- Encourage partnerships across national and cultural boundaries.

- Cooperate with local schools, hospitals, civic organizations, and government agencies to provide comprehensive systems of care for all God's children.

- Establish childcare centers.

- Become informed about childcare conditions existing today and the issues involved in the design of an adequate public policy for childcare.

- Use the appropriate councils and agencies of the church to monitor public policy at federal, state, and local levels of government.

- Become involved in the larger arena of childcare through such organizations as the Children's Defense Fund, the National Association for the Education of Young Children, and the Ecumenical Child-Care Network.

- Celebrate the Children's Sabbath on the second weekend of October.

- Hold study series on needs of children and the poor.

- Offer ongoing tutoring and mentoring programs.

- Offer a drug-prevention program for neighborhood children and youth.

- Send community children to camp along with children of the church.

- Provide a "lending closet" of costly items needed by families.

- Provide transportation to prenatal classes and clinics.

- Establish a food and/or clothing bank.

- Provide a dental health clinic.

- Offer nutrition classes.

Abusive Child Labor

The 2000 General Conference noted that today's children, in too many parts of the world, must not only cope with warfare, famine, and pestilence at an early age but are often denied childhood itself by being forced into labor under abusive and destructive conditions. Many millions of children around the world labor in work that is coerced, forced, bonded, enslaved, or otherwise unfair in wages, injurious to health and safety, and/or obstructive of educational or moral development.

Whereas, the majority of child labor is found in informal sectors of the world's poorest economies, a growing element in global competition is the employment of children in export industries of developing countries. Children work to produce fruit, vegetables, tea, coffee, glass, garments, brassware, leather goods, and hand-knotted carpets for sale on the international market. The Oriental carpet industry employs one of the most abusive forms of bonded child labor, involving perhaps as many as one million children in South Asia.

There is growing awareness in international development agencies that child labor is not a byproduct of generalized poverty, but is rooted in specific policies that disproportionately neglect or disadvantage certain populations—ethnic, caste, or gender groups—and that unbalanced development policies have contributed to the exacerbation of child labor.

Despite child-labor laws, as many as 200,000 children work in agriculture as paid or unpaid labor in the United States. Many children are exposed to pesticides and machinery and are not able to attend school on a regular basis.

The United Nations and the International Labor Organization (ILO) have established universal principles to protect children from such abuse, including the International Covenant on the Rights of the Child and the ILO Convention No. 138 for Minimum Age for Admission to Work. The United States is not a signatory to this international agreement.

What Can a Local Church Do About Child Labor?

■ Urge members of Congress to support public policies that include the ratification and enforcement of international labor conventions regarding child labor.

■ Encourage appropriate agencies and units to join the Child Labor Coalition, a broad-based coalition of medical, welfare, religious, consumer, labor, and human-rights organizations in the United States, and to support such consumer initiatives as the RUGMARK campaign, initiated in India by UNICEF, the South-Asian Coalition on Child Servitude, and others to label and market Oriental carpets made without exploited child labor.

■ Support legislative and administrative measures to enforce bans against the international trafficking in goods made by child labor.

■ Support unilateral and multilateral aid and development policies that attack the root causes of child labor, such as lack of basic education, gender and caste prejudice, and unbalanced development schemes that disadvantage certain populations.

■ Organize a letter-writing campaign to the United States Congress advocating reform of United States labor laws to provide better protection of farm workers' rights and to bring child labor restrictions into conformity with international standards.

Reduce the Risk of Child Sexual Abuse in the Church

While our Christian faith calls us to offer both hospitality and protection to the little ones, churches have not always been safe places for children. Child sexual abuse, exploitation, and ritual abuse occur in churches, both large and small, urban and rural. The problem cuts across all economic, cultural, and racial lines.

Such incidents are devastating to all who are involved—the child, the family, the local church, and its leaders. Increasingly, churches are torn apart by the legal, emotional, and monetary consequences of litigation following allegations of abuse.

God calls us to make our churches safe places, protecting children and other vulnerable persons from sexual and ritual abuse. God calls us to create communities of faith where children and adults can grow safe and strong.

What Can a Local Church Do About Sexual Abuse?

■ Use the book *Safe Sanctuaries,* by Joy Thornburg Melton, as a guide to make sure your church is a safe place for children. Sponsor before/after

29

school programs that provide a safe haven. Require all prospective employees and volunteers to complete an application form plus a written authorization for background screening.

■ Develop and implement an ongoing education plan for the congregation and its leaders on the reality of child abuse, risk factors leading to child abuse, and strategies for prevention.

■ If an accusation is made, inform the district superintendent immediately. Enlist trained support persons to care for the alleged victim and the victim's parents, and other students and church members as needed. Remove the accused from any involvement with children until the situation is resolved.

■ Develop and implement safety procedures for church activities, such as having two or more non-related adults present in the classroom or activity; leaving doors open and installing half-doors or windows in doors; providing hall monitors; instituting sign-in and sign-out procedures for children ages ten or younger; and assuring adequate supervision.

■ Provide "safe corridors" for children walking to and from school.

■ Advise children and young persons of an agency or a person outside as well as within the local church whom they can contact for advice and help if they have suffered abuse.

■ Carry liability insurance that includes sexual abuse coverage.

■ Assist the development of awareness and self-protection skills for children and youth through special curriculum and activities.

■ Be familiar with annual conference and other church policies regarding clergy sexual misconduct. Complete regular audits to determine that policies are implemented.

Teaching Plan

1. Recall and discuss childhood impressions and memories of church. Ask: What person or events were most important in your early understanding of God and Jesus? What does this tell you about contemporary children and their faith development? In what ways do you personally shape any child's understanding of the love of God and issues of faith?

2. Read about the current state of children and poverty. Ask participants to make a list of the things that contribute to the healthy development of children. Ask: What on the list does your church now provide? What could or should your church do to insure the welfare of children in your community?

3. Compare the biblical teaching about children found in Mark 9:33-37 with that of Mark 10:13-16. Ask: In what ways are these two teachings alike? In what ways are they different?

4. Read 2 Timothy 1:3-7. Paul recalls his debt to his ancestors for his faith and then Timothy's debt to the faith of his mother and grandmother. Discuss how parents have shaped your faith.

5. Consider the children in your community. What conditions in their lives might arouse the indignation of Jesus if he were to walk through your town or city? Who might Jesus hold responsible for the plight of those children? Who might he commend for their efforts? What more can you or your church do?

6. Discuss how children are treated in your worship services. Are they full participants? In what ways?

7. Form a task force to meet with the leaders of a local elementary school. Discover how your congregation can adopt a public school and assist children in their learning tasks.

8. Ask: What is your state doing to protect your children? What legislation is needed?

Local Action Reports

"It all just came together; you just had to ask and keep on asking until you found the right people to do the right thing." That's how Linda Boswell described her church's successful effort to assemble more than 2,000 health kits that will go to displaced people in Angola and perhaps Mozambique, Tajikistan, Armenia, or Kosovo.

Linda is the chairperson of the mission team at Northbrook United Methodist Church in Roswell, Georgia. Early in the year, they decided to do a health kit. Not knowing what a realistic goal would be, they just picked a number: 2,001. They would try and assemble 2,001 health kits for the UMCOR Depot that would be sent wherever they were most needed.

How were they going to raise enough money and material donations to assemble 2,001 kits? (That's 2,001 bars of soap, hand towels, washcloths, nail files, combs, toothbrushes, tubes of toothpaste, and 12,006 bandages!) Linda's husband Jim got on the phone and started contacting corporations to see if they could get some of the items donated. He was able to get all the toothbrushes, toothpaste, nail files, combs, and many of the bandages through corporate donations. The congregation worked together to raise the rest. One man bought most of the soap and the washcloths. They found a company that would sell them hand towels at 30 cents each. The Boy Scout troop at the church collected thousands of bandages. The congregation raised $786 through a communion-rail offering, and children and adults of the congregation filled in the gaps with items that were still needed. They surpassed their goal and ended up with enough supplies to assemble 2,289 health kits.

First United Methodist Church in Cedar Falls, Iowa, is the home of Chippy, a Chimpanzee who doesn't know he is a puppet. Chippy knows he's a Chimpanzee, but he thinks that this is an ethnic group, not another species. This is why it bothers him when people refer to him as a monkey. Chippy preaches the children's sermons and shares his insights into the Christian faith with the children who gather around him and the pastor on Sundays. Chippy also has his own Web site *(www.churchchimp.com)*.

In 1994, John Foley, a youth pastor at Park Avenue United Methodist Church in Minneapolis, started DinoMights, a hockey team composed of Latino, Asian

American, Native American, and African American boys and girls from economically disadvantaged families.

DinoMights is more than a hockey team. It is a program that includes tutoring (kids must keep up their grades in order to play on the team); computer instruction; and participating in community service projects. Team members also participate in the congregational life of the church and take camping trips during the summer.

In 1993, the West Ohio Conference of the United Methodist Church started Cornerstone United Methodist Church in an affluent suburban community outside Cincinnati. The congregation decided that ministering to youth would be its top priority. A house on church property was converted into a youth center. The house now includes a cardboard cutout of Superman who welcomes youth at the door, while cutouts of Albert Einstein and the Three Stooges wait in the living room. The walls are mounted with car grilles and traffic signs. In keeping with the theme, the church also launched a Sunday night coffeehouse for youth called "The Road Kill Café." With an average of nearly 100 teens, the Sunday morning gathering has outgrown the house. Youth now hold Sunday morning services in a nearby portable modular unit. Volunteers and staff now hope to build a facility to accommodate 1,500 kids a week.

The Life Skills Ministry at St. James United Methodist Church in Coffeyville, Kansas, includes an after-school program that teaches about the Bible and offers training in cooking, sewing, computer, piano, and crafts, plus tutoring in spelling, reading, math, and social studies. Retired persons teach most of the classes.

Since 1996, the Iowa Annual Conference of The United Methodist Church has sponsored Mobile United Methodist Missionaries that hold Bible schools in parks, town halls, open grassy spaces, community buildings, small churches, and trailer parks. The volunteers have taken the gospel to over 1,500 children. The group also sponsors a summer camp for at-risk children. At camp they ride horses, swim, fish, sing, and make crafts. Through the camping program, they learn of God's unconditional love.

Since 1999, Sidewalk Sunday School has been a life-changing summer project for poor children in several North Dakota cities. On any given afternoon or evening, a 6-by-12-foot trailer with a fold-down stage arrives in a neighborhood. In addition to puppet shows, children are invited to play games, participate in wacky skits, learn Bible verses and stories, make crafts, pray, and grow in their Christian faith.

The Virginia Conference of The United Methodist Church sponsored a January 2002 march to the state capitol in Richmond. Almost 500 people gathered at Centenary United Methodist Church in Richmond to dance, sing, and pray. They then marched to the statehouse where they asked lawmakers for funding for guidance counselors in every public school in the state. Bishop Joe E. Pennel, Jr. urged legislators to listen to the needs of poor working families who need more help with childcare.

Chapter 3

Global
Graying

(Stephen B. Wall-Smith and Joy A. M. Lawler contributed to this chapter.)

Social Principle ¶162E, "Rights of the Aging"

In a society that places primary emphasis upon youth, those growing old in years are frequently isolated from the mainstream of social existence. We support social policies that integrate the aging into the life of the total community, including sufficient incomes, increased and nondiscriminatory employment opportunities, educational and service opportunities, and adequate medical care and housing within existing communities. We urge social policies and programs, with emphasis on the unique concerns of older women and ethnic persons, that ensure to the aging the respect and dignity that is their right as senior members of the human community. Further, we urge increased consideration for adequate pension systems by employers, with provisions for the surviving spouse.

Core Bible Passages

Genesis 18:1-18; Exodus 3:1-12; Acts 9:36-42

For some time, demographic trends have pointed toward inexorable, large-scale "graying" of populations around the world, particularly in developed countries like the United States and Japan. There are now 600 million people over age 60. By 2025, there will be 1.2 billion, with more than 70 percent of those living in developing nations.

Consider these other statistics from the Economics and Statistics Administration of the US Department of Commerce:

- During the twentieth century, the number of persons in the United States under age 65 has tripled, while the number age 65 or over has increased *elevenfold.*

- One in 25 Americans was 65 or older in 1900. In 1994, the ratio was 1 in 8. Projections suggest that 1 in 5 Americans could be over age 65 by 2050.

■ Every day in the United States 5,600 people celebrate their sixty-fifth birthday, and 4,550 persons, 65 years or older, die. The result is an increase of 1,050 older adults per day.

■ Not only is the number of persons over 65 increasing, making up an ever larger part of the US population, but even the elderly as a category are aging. From 1960 to 1994, the number of elderly persons 85 and older increased almost threefold, while the number of persons 65 and over doubled. The "oldest old" constitutes 10 percent of the elderly and a little more than 1 percent of the general population today. However, those numbers are expected to change to 24 percent of the elderly and 5 percent of the population as a whole during the next 50 years.

Increased life expectancy is an important factor in global aging. Susanne Paul, a United Methodist layperson and former executive with the Board of Global Ministries who founded the organization Global Action on Aging in 1994, writes that "life spans have increased even more" in less-developed countries than they have in the US, "doubling in China, Malaysia, Morocco, and Venezuela."

Peter G. Peterson asserts in the book *Gray Dawn: How the Coming Age Wave Will Transform America—and the World* that "global life expectancies have grown more over the last 50 years than over the previous 5,000. Perhaps two thirds of all the people who have ever lived to the age of 65 are alive today."

While global aging is an established fact, how it should be answered remains an open question. Some see worldwide graying as a threat. Others see it as a challenge or an occasion for ministry opportunities.

Fearful Rumblings

Peterson sketches bleak social and economic prospects for developed nations unless governments and citizens begin to prepare seriously and soon for changing demographics. "There's an iceberg dead ahead," he writes. "It's called global aging, and it threatens to bankrupt the great powers. . . . Hardly any country is doing what it should to prepare. Hardly any country is doing much at all. Yet, year after year the crisis approaches with the measurable certainty of an advancing tidal wave."

The "crisis" is first and foremost a financial one. Developed countries have written generous, publicly funded promises to retirees into their social contracts.

Soon, he argues, it will be impossible or untenable to keep those promises; though breaking them will have dire consequences, both for those who must break them as well as for those whose expectations are betrayed. "Today the ratio of working taxpayers to non-working pensioners in the developed world is around 3 to 1. By 2030, absent reform, this ratio will fall to 1.5 to 1—and in some countries, such as Germany and Italy, it will drop all the way down to 1 to 1 or even lower." In other words, soon every working person will be carrying not only his or her own economic load but that of a retired person as well.

Susanne Paul suggests that present structures may collapse long before the burden on working persons reaches that point. "Nation states have not continued to grow," she writes. "For at least ten years and perhaps more, states have been weakening, putting the future of older citizens in serious question. In a rapidly globalizing world economy, with free movement of capital and exploding offshore tax havens . . . governments are losing their taxing capacity. Budgets are cut, and older persons are often the targets."

Peterson ponders other implications of global aging. The rate of saving, for example, is a traditional engine of economic growth. What will happen to capital markets when savings dry up? How much deficit spending on health care is likely to be considered justifiable? How will senior-focused public spending affect other institutions, such as public schools? What will cars be like when most drivers are over 50? What are the national defense implications for a population with more senior citizens than young people?

Neither Peterson nor Paul considers the future to be a relentless downward spiral of "graying and paying," *if* policymakers, political leaders, and ordinary citizens take heed and take action right away. Among proposals Peterson makes are later retirement, means testing for publicly funded pensions such as social security, pro-natal, and pro-immigration policies (to increase the number of younger workers in developed economies), and concerted efforts to keep elder care primarily a family, rather than a public, responsibility.

Active Older Adults in the Bible

We commonly hold that biblical cultures were more respectful of older persons than is often the case today (see, for example, Proverbs 16:31), though that may not be completely true. On the one hand, elders were certainly to be respected within their extended family units (see Exodus 20:12). On the other hand, the situation of persons without families (such as widows and orphans) might well become desperate whether they were aged or not.

Many of the characters in the readings that follow are aged, though in every case, their ages turn out to be irrelevant to the challenges put before them. Genesis 18:1-18 tells of the angels' visit to Abraham and Sarah, during the course of which they announced that the couple surely would bear a child together, a child who would become a major player in God's covenant with humankind. The couple was skeptical but willing to be part of whatever God required.

Similarly, in Exodus 3:1-12 God called an 80-year-old Moses at the burning bush and sent him to free the people of Israel. In fact, Moses had made premature gestures in that direction when he was younger and found himself an exile. Only when he was older and wiser was he suited to the work that God gave him. Read further and notice that while Moses made a number of excuses as he attempted to elude God's call, his advanced age was not one of them.

We don't really know the age of the disciple Dorcas (or Tabitha) whose charity was lauded in Acts 9:36-42. We presume that because she spent so much time and energy on poor widows in the Christian community, she was one of them and was elderly herself at the time she died. In any event, she had a wonderful ministry in which skills polished over a lifetime were highly valued. Not only was she not allowed to take a passive retirement, she also was not even, for the moment anyway, permitted to die!

Rethinking the Life Cycle

Peterson notes that in order to make proposals such as his palatable, persons of all ages—the elderly included—need to rethink commonly accepted views of aging. Nothing else will change until we change our ideas about the human life cycle. In this view, he echoes Julia Alvarez, a UN ambassador from the Dominican Republic, who said, "Perception precedes politics. The image of older people as full, useful, and active citizens must become firmly implanted in the popular imagination."

No one has to look far to find examples of older adults who are retired but not retiring. Alta Merritt Richardson, 83, lives in Indianapolis, Indiana, where she is a member of North United Methodist Church. She says her life is busy and rewarding. She works as a tutor and volunteer teacher's aide at two schools, looks after a ten-year-old boy one evening a week, spends time with homebound persons as a service to family caregivers, provides transportation to those who no longer drive, and remains active in her church. She serves on the worship and parish-development committees. She also writes letters to all first-time church visitors (more than 350 at last count) as well as notes to those unable to leave home, leads a weekly prayer group, and is a mainstay of the Stuffers Club, assisting with the bimonthly mailing of the church newsletter.

The nice thing about this season in her life, Richardson says, is that "you're able to do the things you want to do—for me that is doing the things for other people that need to be done. It makes you feel so much better for having done it." She says that seniors add important traits to the mix of interests in churches and other groups, including "experience in life, tolerance and openness, patience, stability, and roots."

She admits, however, that older adults sometimes find it a challenge to get younger persons to receive their gifts. "The younger ones don't think the older ones know much," she said. "Seniors think nobody wants the benefit of their knowledge." She pointed to a paucity of "older people serving in positions of meaningful leadership" as evidence. "Most of the older folks think they are the forgotten generation," she said, "which they are."

Bobbie Kingsbury, 67, of Whites Creek, Tennessee, is another senior who has become deeply involved in her community since retiring. She is a mentor in Cool School, an after-school program supported by Beech Grove United Methodist Church, where Bobbie is a member. She thinks her mentoring not only helps students to succeed but also helps to break down limiting images of different generations. "The stereotype is that older people are intolerant," she said; "but the truth is that as you get older, you learn to accept each person individually and not expect everyone to be cut from the same mold. You learn to accept them for what they are, regardless of what they can or can't do, or the way they live."

Susanne Paul writes, "We must work to forge a new society built for an aging population that will welcome all of us in our later years." She notes that one of the UN's standards for social development is the number of people in a country aged 60 and above. "It's a benchmark," she said in a recent speech, "an indicator of a good society."

How "Senior Friendly" Is Your Church?

The "friendliness" of a church is not only measured by the sociability of its staff and membership but also by the *accessibility* of its facilities and the *inclusiveness* of its programs. Accessibility and inclusiveness may mean different things to different age groups.

For older persons, accessibility includes such things as number and height of stairs, availability of ramps and elevators, width and weight of doors, distance between the sanctuary and facilities used for education and fellowship, proximity of parking and restrooms to commonly used areas in the church, availability of handrails, and the condition of walking surfaces indoors and out. Waxed floors that are slippery when wet can be difficult for some seniors to manage as can gravel or flagstone parking areas and walkways. Good-quality amplification systems should be fitted to the rooms where they are used. Extraneous noise, such as that from heating and air-conditioning units, should be limited because it garbles other sounds when picked up by hearing aids.

Inclusive programs allow older adults to make significant contributions to their churches and communities in keeping with their interests and abilities. Audit the opportunities that seniors have to take leadership roles in worship, education, and outreach. Are older adults a focus of evangelism, or are all recruiting efforts centered on young families? Congregations should beware of hidden messages that belittle seniors. These might include the scheduling of events exclusively in the evening (in order to accommodate working adults but not *older* adults who may be unable to drive at night); the use of worship innovations that appeal only to young people; or the use of graphics that equate "family" with *"young* family." A billboard outside a Missouri church, for example, declares itself "family friendly" and displays a silhouette of a young couple with two small children.

Teaching Plan

*1. **Read the statistics*** in the introduction to this section and "Fearful Rumblings" (pages 36–37). Discuss any information that surprises group members. Determine the group's awareness of demographic changes and the extent to which the "graying" of society has affected them already. Ask: What evidence in your life or in your community do you see for the aging of our population? Is popular culture reflecting this change? What examples can you name?

*2. **Discuss global aging.*** On a piece of posterboard, write the words "threat," "challenge," and "opportunity." By a show of hands, determine group members' general sense of what global aging represents. Ask members to explain briefly their positions.

"In The United Methodist Church today, approximately 62 percent of its membership is 50 years and older." Ask: What does this mean for the church?

*3. **Brainstorm images*** of what "getting older" means to them. Record the images on a chalkboard or a piece of posterboard. Compare the number of negative images (such as "arthritis" or "memory loss") to the number of positive images ("wisdom" or "contentment").

*4. **Read "Rethinking the Life Cycle"*** (pages 38–39). Discuss the profiles of active seniors contained in the study guide. Do you agree that praising these and other older adults like them is a tacit admission that we expect other, less-flattering stereotypes to define older persons?

*5. **Create.*** Using construction paper and other art supplies, have group members create "lifelines" (visual records of their own lives, beginning with birth and ending with a speculative year of death). Explain that they should represent milestones such as births of siblings, conversion, marriage, births of children, deaths of parents, and so on. Allow group members to share their creations, explaining their symbols.

Reflect on the nature of the milestones group members record. How many of them represent traumatic, unexpected incidents? How many represent predictable transitions from one stage of life to another? Do the lifelines reflect an image of their old age as primarily stable and static or as unpredictable and full of significant events? Ask: What milestones are still to come in your life? When you look at the whole span of your life, as you conceive it, what elements change from one period to another? What remains constant?

6. ***Read Genesis 18:1-18, Exodus 3:1-12, Acts 9:36-42, and "Active Older Adults in the Bible"*** (pages 37–38). Form three small groups if desirable. Discuss these passages and what they have to say about the way God works in the lives of older persons. Ask: How relevant is age to full participation in the kingdom of God? In your experience, are there unique ways that God speaks through older persons? What are they? Can you cite any examples from your congregation? from your own family?"

How closely does your church conform to the denomination as a whole (with about 62 percent of its membership being 50 years and older)? What does this mean for the church?

7. ***Read "How 'Senior Friendly' Is Your Church?"*** (pages 39–40). Discuss the "senior friendliness" of your own local church. Be specific. Ask: What features of your building or your practice of ministry may make it difficult for some older adults to participate fully? In what ways do you minister well with older adults? To what extent are older adults full participants in the life of the congregation? To what extent are they excluded or "ghettoized"?

8. ***Ask:*** What are some differences between ministries *to* or *for* older adults and ministries *with* older persons? What opportunities for ministry with seniors has your church taken? What other opportunities are open?

9. ***Consider your congregation and its resources.*** Take a moment to brainstorm particular needs for older adults in your church or community that your congregation might address. Make a list. Select one and then write a mission statement for starting a new ministry with older people in your congregation.

Local Action Reports

The Reverend Dr. Elbert C. Cole takes every opportunity to confront and overturn myths about aging. "We've said goodbye to a youth-oriented society," Cole said. "The age wave is the cutting edge." The retired United Methodist pastor—himself an extraordinarily energetic and active senior—is a co-founder and executive director of Shepherd's Centers of America in Kansas City, Missouri, an interfaith agency that helps congregations organize and operate ministries with older adults.

Cole emphasizes the word *with*; part of what makes the 100 or so Shepherd's Centers located across the US unique and effective is their emphasis on seniors working as "helpers and healers" for other older adults. Shepherd's Centers do not focus on passive recreational activities that are sometimes offered as "ministry to seniors."

"People want purpose in their lives," Cole said recently, "not to be entertained. Their minds are active. They don't want to be pampered or demeaned."

The first Shepherd's Center was planted in 1972, after a three-year study of 75-year-olds revealed that the most compelling issues in their lives were not boredom or poor health but finding suitable outlets for energy, skills, and interests. Many had been satisfied in their careers and had been uncertain, since retirement, what their role and function in society and their changing families might still be. "These are faith questions," Cole said, "pointing to central issues of meaning and hope. People seek stimulation of mind and spirit. They want to understand more deeply. In the Genesis story, God created life and called it good. There's nothing in the story about the warranty expiring at 65." Cole notes that 80 percent of seniors are independent and healthy; others need only modest help with activities of daily living. At any given moment, he says, only 5 percent of people over 65 are in nursing homes, a figure that has stayed constant for many years.

A typical Shepherd's Center program includes educational activities, such as lectures and short courses on topics of interest to participants; exercise, health, and fitness classes; social activities and outings; and organized service opportunities, which may include such things as home maintenance, Meals on Wheels, companion services, and respite care.

A statement entitled "The Ten Characteristics of a Shepherd's Center" affirms that "a Shepherd's Center is a new social model informed by a healthy view of life after retirement, providing new benchmarks for vital involvement and significant and meaningful living in later years. The concept is believed to be applicable to any ethnic, economic, or cultural group of older adults. It takes a commitment of people helping people to live meaningful lives."

A United Methodist program offering travel and service opportunities for older adults made its debut in January 2002. The Primetimers Program of the denomination's Board of Global Ministries, designed for people age 50 and older, integrates educational and cultural experiences with Christian service. The board scheduled more than a dozen events for 2002. Most events cost $300 to $500, which covers room, meals, local transportation, program, and insurance. For information call 877-882-4724 or visit the Web site *primetimers@gbgm-umc.org*.

Each year during the second week in September, a group of older adults in Washington State spends three days at Lazy Daze Camp and Retreat Center. Members enjoy getting to know others from around the state, hiking, workshops, campfires, great food, and other outdoor and relational experiences.

Older adult members of Edmonds (Washington) United Methodist Church also participate in an "On the Move" choir that meets to sing hymns and other favorite songs. The choir also sings at nursing homes and rehab centers. The church sponsors Emanons, a group of adults in its 70s and 80s who gather once a month for special events such as plays or concerts. The church also has a Golden Years group that meets regularly for potluck luncheons and Saturday Niters who meet once a month for special events. Finally, a group of Senior Singles get together on the first Sunday of each month following worship and go out to eat at a nearby restaurant. Edmonds created ministries to meet the needs of its older members. An "On-the-Move" choir was formed for seniors who love music. The group sings beloved hymns and favorite songs for residents of nursing homes and retirement centers.

The United Methodist Church in Santa Rosa, California, sponsors OASIS (Older Adult Singles in Support). The group was established in 1986 so older single adults could support one another and enjoy social activities together. The group meets on the first and third Wednesdays of each month. Meetings include group discussions, speakers, lunches, and field trips.

Chapter 4

Women in Changing Roles

(Pamela Dilmore contributed to this chapter.)

Social Principle ¶162F, "Rights of Women"

We affirm women and men to be equal in every aspect of their common life. We therefore urge that every effort be made to eliminate sex-role stereotypes in activity and portrayal of family life and in all aspects of voluntary and compensatory participation in the Church and society. We affirm the right of women to equal treatment in employment, responsibility, promotion, and compensation. We affirm the importance of women in decision-making positions at all levels of Church life and urge such bodies to guarantee their presence through policies of employment and recruitment. We support affirmative action as one method of addressing the inequalities and discriminatory practices within our church and society. We urge employers of persons in dual career families, both in the Church and society, to apply proper consideration of both parties when relocation is considered.

Core Bible Passages

Philippians 2:1-5; Luke 12:16-20; and John 15:1-17

According to the AFL-CIO women who work full-time are paid only *73 cents* weekly for every dollar men earn, and women of color who work full-time are paid only *64 cents* for every dollar men earn overall.

It is true that wage gaps between men and women have declined steadily in recent decades, though progress slowed in the 1990s. Today's wage gap is 10 percentage points lower than it was in 1979, when women earned only 63 cents for every dollar men earned, and the gap was 37 percent.

The narrowing of the gender wage gap since 1979 might indicate less progress than appears on the surface. Over the past two decades, most of the reduction in the wage gap was due to the decline in men's wages—not because women's wages were rising. Falling wages for men accounted for roughly half of the decline in the gender wage gap between 1979 and 1989 and for a stunning four-fifths of the decline between 1989 and 1997. Pay bias and discriminatory practices persist and continue to slow the closing of the gap.

In 1963, Congress passed the Equal Pay Act, which outlawed the standard business practice of paying women less than men even when they were doing exactly the same work. The mandate was straightforward: equal pay for equal work. However, other forms of discrimination, including setting lower wages for "women's jobs," continue to depress wages for women. Pay equity is the term more often used to describe the remedy for wage discrimination against women— or equal pay for work of equal value.

Some people argue that the wage gap is due to women's choices (such as the choice to have children or act as caregiver). They claim that when education and experience are the same, the wage gap disappears. Although there is some validity to this claim, recent studies show that between one-quarter and one-half of the gender wage gap remains unexplained even after taking differences in education and experience into account. Many economists attribute some or all of this unexplained portion of the wage gap to discrimination.

Another phenomenon is the depressing impact women present in any form of employment. As the percentage of women rises in any occupational group, wages tend to decline. Workers who do what traditionally has been viewed as "women's work—clerical workers, cashiers, librarians, childcare workers, and others in jobs in which 70 percent or more of the workers are women—typically earn less than workers in jobs that are predominately male or are integrated by gender. As a result, the 25.6 million women who work in female-dominated jobs receive an average of $3,446 less in annual income than if they were employed in fields not dominated by women. This fact also adversely affects men. Four million men who work in predominately female occupations receive an average of $6,259 less than they would if they were employed in other occupations.

Women and Education

Women now outnumber men at most graduation ceremonies.

According to Thomas Mortenson, an Iowa-based researcher in higher education, in 1996, 55.1 percent of bachelor's degrees were awarded to women. Women now earn 200,000 more bachelor's degrees a year than men, and some colleges are now using affirmative action that favors men for admissions.

In Kansas City, for example, 62 percent of its 1997 master's degrees went to women and in Missouri 57 percent of the degrees went to women. The gender gap is even wider between black women and men. Nationwide, in 1997, black women earned 60 percent of all bachelors' degrees and 65 percent of all masters' degrees awarded to black students. White women earned 57 percent of all bachelors' degrees awarded to whites.

Apparently then, women are finding opportunities in higher education. Women with skills and education are quickly rising to the top in many fields. Overall, however, the gender gap still favors men and the women who choose to remain in the workforce rather than women who take time out to raise children or attend to family needs. Many more women than men still opt to be the stay-at-home parent. Do working women have as much freedom to determine their parenting/career balance as men do? For example, are men given enough paternity leave from their workplaces to allow them to take up a role as primary caregiver? Are women who take time off from work to rear their children unfairly penalized when they go back to work?

Changing Family Roles

One of the effects of the Industrial Revolution was that men were separated from women. Men went to work in factories while women generally stayed home. The revolution also separated fathers from their children and contributed to an erosion of respect for the uncompensated labor of women in the home.

On the other hand, industrialization also offered new economic, political, and educational opportunities for women and contributed to the decrease of labor by women in the home with such inventions as washing machines, vacuum cleaners, and refrigerators.

Welfare, introduced in 1935, was designed to offer financial support that would permit women to stay at home with their children rather than become wage earners. An unintended consequence of this policy was that among the poor, unemployed males became unaffordable, unnecessary, and unwanted.

Today, at a time that sees men engaging in new childcare roles, many men are absent from the parenting role entirely. In 1996, 21.2 percent of all US children were being reared in single-mother households; and in 1994–95, more than 30 percent of all US children were born to unmarried women. The income disparity between men and women, plus the loss of two incomes to support the household, assures that most children living in single-parent households will live in poverty. It is the combination of these factors that produces a poverty rate for children in the United States that is approaching 25 percent.

What Do Women Think?

What is the perception of women in the United States regarding such signs of change? Do they still feel a gender gap in the ability to forge ahead in careers and to make a salary that justly compensates them for their training and skills? *Minneapolis-St. Paul Magazine* (May 1999) published results of a phone survey of women in the seven-county metro area and a roundtable discussion that asked for opinions and feelings of women on a variety of topics. The survey revealed that 81 percent of the women did not feel that sexism had hindered their lives.

Of these women, 68 percent with master's degrees and 57 percent with doctorates did not see sexism as a hindrance to progress in their careers.

Teaching Plan

1. Read aloud Philippians 2:1-5. Allow a moment of silence. Ask: What images stand out for you in the Scripture? What does the Scripture say to you about human relationships?

2. Pray the following: "Thank you, God, for creating us, men and women, in your image. Thank you for the gifts you have given us. Help us explore and celebrate our potential. Forgive us when our attitudes create boundaries or obstacles that prevent others and ourselves from growing as you intend. Open our hearts as we explore the changing roles of women and men in our culture. In the name of Christ we pray."

3. Consider men and women. Divide the group by gender. Provide separate chalkboards or posterboard for both groups. Ask each group to write the words "male" and "female" at the top of two columns. Have participants think of traits or actions that are considered to be male or female; write these in the appropriate columns. Go through the list together and ask: Did men and women give different answers? Do you see traits in the male column that you would also write in the female column or vice versa? What does this activity say about the cultural perceptions of men and women?

4. Ask: Do women have the same opportunity to rise to managerial and executive positions? Are women penalized professionally for taking time off to raise children? Is this fair? Are maternity and paternity leave allowances adequate to insure fairness between men and women?

5. Team study. Form two teams. Assign the first team to read "Women and Education" (pages 46–47). Assign the second team to read "Changing Family Roles" (pages 47–48). Ask the teams to answer the following questions: What surprises you about the information? What questions emerge as a result of reading this? What does this section say to you about the changing roles of men and women? How does your faith help you sort through some of the issues raised? Choose a leader and report your findings to the whole group.

6. Read "What Do Women Think?" (page 48). Ask: What key challenges lie ahead for women or men? Are you excited or threatened by these changes? Why? Do you think men or women have the upper hand in America today? In what ways?

7. Close by singing "All Praise to Our Redeeming Lord" as a closing prayer.

Local Action Report

In 1996, 12 women in a United Methodist Church in Bellaire, Texas, started women's Outreach to Women (WOW). Prior to the establishment of WOW, the church sponsored Boy Scout troops, but now the church is a meeting place for five Girl Scout troops.

The group sponsors spiritual retreats for the women of the church, and it has conducted a four-part "Career Interest Assessment" for early teens. Men and women serving as mechanics, orthodontists, chemists, commercial designers, and office managers spoke to the groups. WOW also conducted two community seminars for women on physical, spiritual, and emotional well-being. The active group also financially supports the Heifer Project and two residential facilities for women who are abused or are recovering from chemical dependency.

In May 2001, WOW was honored with a Peace and Justice Award by the Texas Conference for its work with "Ten Thousand Villages," a non-profit consignment store selling products from artisans from Houston and around the world. "Seventy percent of the artisans are women supporting themselves and their children," says Cathy Helms, a WOW volunteer. The store also sells products from over 200 work cooperatives in over 45 countries. The cooperatives represent work groups of various faiths, and many offer employment to young girls who might otherwise turn to prositution. The project also provides a way for persons living with AIDS or handicapping conditions to support themselves.

Helms says the next project for WOW is to educate people about the global trafficking of women and children

Chapter 5

America's Favorite Legal Drug

(John William Peterson and Melissa L. Lauber
contributed to this chapter.)

Social Principle ¶162J, "Alcohol and Other Drugs"

We affirm our long-standing support of abstinence from alcohol as a faithful witness to God's liberating and redeeming love for persons. We support abstinence from the use of any illegal drugs. Since the use of alcohol and illegal drugs is a major factor in crime, disease, death, and family dysfunction, we support educational programs encouraging abstinence from such use.

Millions of living human beings are testimony to the beneficial consequences of therapeutic drug use, and millions of others are testimony to the detrimental consequences of drug misuse. We encourage wise policies relating to the availability of potentially beneficial or potentially damaging prescription and over-the-counter drugs; we urge that complete information about their use and misuse be readily available to both doctor and patient. We support the strict administration of laws regulating the sale and distribution of all opiates. We support regulations that protect society from users of drugs of any kind where it can be shown that a clear and present social danger exists. Drug-dependent persons and their family members are individuals of infinite human worth deserving of treatment, rehabilitation, and ongoing life-changing recovery. Misuse should be viewed as a symptom of underlying disorders for which remedies should be sought. We commit ourselves to assisting those who have become dependent, and their families, in finding freedom through Jesus Christ and in finding good opportunities for treatment, for ongoing counseling, and for reintegration into society.

Social Principle ¶162K, "Tobacco"

We affirm our historic tradition of high standards of personal discipline and social responsibility. In light of the overwhelming evidence that tobacco smoking and the use of smokeless tobacco are hazardous to the health of persons of all ages, we recommend total abstinence from the use of tobacco. We urge that our educational and communication resources be utilized to support and encourage such abstinence. Further, we recognize the harmful effects of passive smoke and support the restriction of smoking in public areas and workplaces.

Core Bible Passages

Genesis 9:18-27, 19:30-38; Matthew 11:18-19; Matthew 26:26-29; John 2:9-11; Romans 13:13; 1 Corinthians 5:11-13; 1 Timothy 3:2-3; Titus 1:7; 1 Corinthians 6:9-10; Galatians 5:19-21; 1 Peter 4:3

It was supposed to be a celebration. Benjamin Wynne, 20, had received his pledge pin; and in the hallowed tradition of his new fraternity, Louisiana State University's Sigma Alpha Epsilon, he proceeded to get blasted. First, his frat brothers took him to an off-campus kegger where Benjamin began "funneling" beer shot through a rubber hose straight into his mouth. Next, they moved to a bar where they knocked down "Three Wise Men," a potent drink of 151-proof rum, Crown Royal whiskey, and Jagermeister liqueur.

The festivities ended with the upperclassmen wheeling home the drunken pledges in shopping carts, since they were far too intoxicated to walk. Wynne "was staggering," said one eyewitness, "but no more than a lot of other people." When police were finally called later that night, they found nearly two dozen young men passed out on the living room floor of the fraternity house. By the next morning, Benjamin was dead of alcohol poisoning. An autopsy revealed he had a blood alcohol concentration six times higher than the state's intoxication level, an equivalent of 24 drinks.

Party On!

Although Wynne's death was just one of several high-profile binge-drinking tragedies in 1997, the situation regarding alcohol abuse on America's campuses has not improved notably since then. Our system of higher education remains drenched in booze. Each year, undergraduates drink four billion cans of beer, an average of 55 six-packs apiece. As you might expect given this volume, they are not quietly sipping a glass of Bordeaux with their brie. Instead, they drink with the expressed intention of getting seriously drunk.

In a pivotal study of binge drinking—defined as five or more drinks in a single outing for men and four or more for women—conducted by Harvard University, researchers found that of the more than 50,000 students surveyed, 44 percent had engaged in binge drinking during the past two weeks. At almost one-third of the colleges surveyed, half of those surveyed admitted to having binged on alcohol three or more times during the past two weeks. Even more disturbing, 62 percent of male binge drinkers and 49 percent of females shared that they had driven while under the influence. The study calculated that binge drinkers were 7 to 16 times more likely than nonbinging students to miss class, fail to complete homework, have unprotected sex, get into a confrontation with police, damage property, and sustain injuries. Not surprisingly, binge drinkers are likely to be white athletes who are members of either a fraternity or a sorority.

Countermeasures

In response to binging tragedies, universities, which had at one time winked at their students' alcohol-infused highjinks, are now attempting to curb alcohol abuse. Most of their effort, as one might expect, has come in the form of educational initiatives, featuring literature and workshops highlighting the dangers of underage drinking. Many are now providing students the opportunity to live in alcohol-free dorms, writing stern letters to the parents of offenders, and banning alcohol from campus activities. Despite their best efforts, no one expects colleges will be able to curb abusive drinking as long as alcohol enjoys its current level of acceptance in society.

"You can have a perfect program on campus," says William DeJong of the Harvard School of Public Health, "but if you don't do anything about the liquor store across the street that sells to minors or the bar that serves intoxicated students, you haven't solved the problem." Indeed, on the night Benjamin died, Louisiana State University had a schoolwide no-alcohol policy in force. Yet neither that fact nor the fact that he was underage, could protect Benjamin from his own excess.

The Cost

The binging that takes place on campuses is a reflection of the United States' acceptance of alcohol abuse, a tolerance for which we pay a heavy price. In one nationwide study, it was found that an average of 30 percent of suicides, 50 percent of homicides, and 50 percent of all criminal offenses involve alcohol use. Alcohol-related deaths outnumber drug-related deaths four to one.

Furthermore, the National Institute on Alcohol Abuse and Alcoholism estimates that the cost of alcohol to our society in the form of hospital expenses, crime, lost productivity, and accidents is over $200 billion a year. Annually, alcohol contributes to 100,000 deaths. The National Highway Traffic Safety Administration reports that there is one fatality nearly every 33 minutes due to alcohol-impaired driving.

Debauchery

The Hebrew Scriptures condemn drunkenness as an abomination. The stories that recount the shame of Noah and Lot (Genesis 9:18-27; 19:30-38) are cautionary tales against intoxication. Proverbs also contains admonitions against overindulgence (Proverbs 20:1; 23:20-21; 31:4-5); while in Hosea, wine is associated with sexual promiscuity (Hosea 4:11b). The prophets condemn the abuse of alcohol by their rulers because of the resulting moral blindness (Isaiah 5:11-12; 56:11-12; Amos 6:4-7). Priests could not partake of wine while on duty in the sanctuary (Leviticus 10:8-9); and in Deuteronomy 21:20, parents of a rebellious son disown him with the words, "He is a glutton and a drunkard."

The New Testament is no more forgiving of drinking to excess than the Hebrew Scriptures. Drunkenness is associated with debauchery and Gentile depravity. Paul appeals to the church in Rome, "Let us live honorably as in the day, not in reveling and drunkenness, not in debauchery and licentiousness" (Romans 13:13).

The writer of First Peter admonishes his audience, "You have already spent enough time in doing what the Gentiles like to do, living in licentiousness, passions, drunkenness, revels, carousing, and lawless idolatry" (1 Peter 4:3). Moreover, a leader in the Christian church had to forgo intemperance. First Timothy contains a list of attributes desired in a bishop, including the statement that a bishop is not to be "a drunkard" (1 Timothy 3:3). The Letter to Titus also specifies that a bishop should not be "addicted to wine" (Titus 1:7). Paul even goes so far as to say that drunkards will not inherit the kingdom of God (1 Corinthians 6:9-10; Galatians 5:19-21), nor are they to be tolerated in the community of faith (1 Corinthians 5:11-13).

Fruit of the Vine

Anyone looking for a blanket condemnation of alcohol in the Scriptures may be disappointed. Instead the biblical message is a bit more ambiguous. Wine, the fruit of the vine, was praised as a gift of God. It seems that Jesus himself occasionally partook. In fact, his critics slandered him as a "glutton and drunkard," an accusation he didn't bother to refute (Matthew 11:19).

At the wedding at Cana (John 2:9-11), Jesus proved himself a connoisseur of fine wine, providing an exceptional vintage when the stores had run dry. And in the final action of the Last Supper (Matthew 26:26-29), he lifted the cup and declared it to be the blood of the new covenant, promising not to "drink of this fruit of the vine" with his disciples until that day when they would all drink together in the kingdom of God. (Many denominations continue to use wine as a part of their celebration of Holy Communion out of deference to the practice of Jesus and his disciples.)

Thus Jesus did not explicitly disapprove of using alcohol. Instead, he drank wine as was the custom of his day. He cautioned, however, against all unhealthy behavior. Otherwise, the thorough vilification of drunkenness by the early Christians is difficult to explain. So it seems that the overall biblical attitude toward the use of alcohol was a stance of cautious moderation rather than of total abstinence.

The Sacred Cow

Despite the pound of flesh it exacts from society, alcohol continues to enjoy a privileged position. Just how privileged can be illustrated by comparing its fortunes with that of the tobacco industry. While Joe Camel has been sent packing, Budweiser continues hawking its product with impunity. In fact, televised sporting events, which have made fans of millions of youngsters, often seem like nothing more than an extolment of the pleasures of alcohol.

No wonder the median age kids start to drink is 13 years old. Even the government seems willing to give the alcoholic beverage producers a free ride. Due to rising government-imposed taxes, the price of a pack of cigarettes has increased 57 percent since 1996. In contrast, the price of a six-pack of beer, when adjusted for inflation, has actually been on the decline since 1991. In addition, government has supported alcohol by its refusal to label it as a "drug."

Despite the lobbying of dozens of groups such as Mothers Against Drunk Driving (MADD), the Clinton administration's drug-control office refused to add alcohol to its $1 billion National Youth Anti-Drug Media Campaign in 1999. The reason? The Office of National Drug-Control Policy limits its definition of *drugs* to "controlled substances," which excludes alcohol. The government's reluctance to categorize alcohol as a "drug" is due in part to fears that such a label would diminish the importance of its fight against what it considers "real drugs," such as marijuana, cocaine, and heroin.

A Bar on Every Corner

Our ambivalence toward alcohol is long-standing. Colonial America was hardly for the weak of liver. The Puritans are said to have carried more beer than water on the *Mayflower*. During our formative years as a nation, it was not uncommon to find a tavern for every 150 to 200 citizens. By the 1830's, the average United States resident drank three times as much as we do today.

As can easily be imagined, public drunkenness and the civil disorder that accompanied it offended the early Methodists. As early as 1783, the Methodist Conference expressed concern about the evils of alcohol: "Should our friends be permitted to make spirituous liquors, sell, and drink them in drams? By no means: we think it wrong in its nature and consequences; and desire all our preachers to teach the people by precept and example to put away this evil."

In time, Methodism would become the driving force behind the Temperance Movement, which sought to outlaw the sale of alcohol in the United States. Methodist Frances E. Willard became president of the Women's Christian Temperance Union. She hoped, with other Prohibition leaders, that in persuading Americans not to drink, there would be a sober nation within about 30 years. Eventually, the fervor of the Temperance Movement was rewarded with the Eighteenth Amendment, which made the sale of alcoholic beverages illegal. Prohibition had begun, but the goal of a dry and sober nation was not to be.

Legacy

The extremes of Prohibition would prove unpopular. In 1933, the law was repealed. Though the pendulum swung back to alcohol use, the legacy of the Temperance Movement continues to influence American society. During the past few decades, the forces of reform have succeeded in raising the legal purchase age of alcohol, placing warning labels on alcoholic beverages, stiffening the penalties for drunk driving, and lowering the legal blood alcohol concentration level. Despite a spike caused by the coming of age of the baby boomers, per capita alcohol consumption has been decreasing since 1980.

The influence of the Temperance Movement is also felt within the alcohol-abuse treatment community. The dominant model of therapy for half a century has been abstinence, a concept dear to Frances Willard's heart. This approach holds that alcohol abuse is a disease and that the only acceptable treatment is to stop drinking. Any other strategy is deemed too risky. "Every alcoholic would like to drink moderately," says Dr. Douglas Talbott, president of the American Society of Addiction Medicine. "Ninety percent have tried. This just feeds into the denial of the alcoholic."

In All Things Moderation

Increasingly, a movement in favor of moderation is challenging the abstinence model of interdiction. The behaviorist proponents of moderation argue that only 5 percent of problem drinkers are alcoholics. About 20 percent of Americans have a problem with their drinking. They drink too much and may even binge on occasion, but they usually don't drink steadily or suffer withdrawals when they stop. For them, the behaviorists argue, abstinence is not needed; instead, a program of treatment called Moderation Management is prescribed. "It's a harm-reduction approach," says Dr. Alan Marlatt, director of the University of Washington's Addictive Behaviors Research Center. Using this approach, he has been able to reduce binge drinking significantly in 80 percent of his patients. "With young people," he adds, "if you only offer abstinence, they're not going to sign up."

The reaction of the abstinence-based treatment community to Moderation Management has been harsh. Moderation proponents stand accused of serving as enablers. "We've been accused of murder," says Marlatt. In return, the moderates argue that the abstinence crowd's "all or nothing" approach is too legalistic. At this point, the moderates appear to be outmatched. After all, Moderation Management has just 50 volunteer-run groups, while Alcoholics Anonymous has an estimated 1.2 million members. But the moderates are a spunky bunch. "We're like booze revolutionaries," says Elisa DeCarlo, who directs a weekly Moderation Management meeting in Manhattan.

The United Methodist Position

The abuse of alcohol and other drugs has reached global proportions. More alcohol and other drugs are produced and consumed than ever before. In consuming countries, with their attendant problems of poverty, racism, domestic violence, hopelessness, and material despair, alcohol and other drug abuse is a part of a continuing cycle of economic and spiritual turmoil.

Abuse of legal drugs (alcohol, tobacco, and pharmaceuticals) remains a leading cause of disease and death around the world. While recreational use of illegal drugs in the United States has declined, the use of drugs remains socially acceptable as levels of addiction and abuse continue to rise.

Growing numbers of cities, small towns, and rural areas around the world are caught in a web of escalating alcohol and other drug-related violence. As the findings of the regional hearings in the United States stressed: "Drug addiction crosses all ethnic, cultural, and economic backgrounds." Social systems are dangerously strained under the heavy weight of alcohol and other drug-related health and social problems. Meanwhile, the supply of drugs from developing countries continues to grow in response to high demand from the developed countries.

The United States policy response to the drug crisis has focused almost exclusively on law enforcement and military solutions. This policy, in some cases, has led to the erosion of precious civil liberties and human rights, especially for poor and minority communities. International strategies should reflect the need for balanced, equitable economic growth and stable democratic governments in drug-producing developing countries. Most important, any alternative strategy must be rooted in local communities. The most creative and effective approaches to the present crisis begins at the local level.

The United Methodist Church has long opposed abuse of alcohol and other drugs. In 1916, the General Conference authorized the formation of a Board of Temperance, Prohibition, and Public Morals "to make more effectual the efforts of the church to create public sentiment and crystallize the same into successful opposition to the organized traffic in intoxicating liquors."

In response to the alcohol and other drug crisis, The United Methodist Church is committed to a holistic approach, which emphasizes prevention, intervention, treatment, community organization, public advocacy, and abstinence. Out of love for God and our neighbors, the church must have a positive role by offering a renewed spiritual perspective on this crisis.

United Methodists Try to Unsaddle the Marlboro Man

In 1996, the General Conference of the United Methodist Church expressed concern about the marketing practices of Philip Morris, which sells Marlboro cigarettes, and RJR Nabisco, which sells Camel cigarettes.

The assembly asked the United Methodist General Board of Church and Society (GBCS) to "explore productive measures aimed at stopping tobacco companies from marketing cigarettes and other tobacco products to children, and, if necessary, organize a boycott."

After studying the issue and unsuccessfully working with the cigarette manufacturers, in March 2001, the board joined a boycott of Kraft Foods and its Philip Morris subsidiary. That boycott is led by INFACT, a group of organizations that was first organized to lead a boycott against Nestle products. INFACT had been pressuring Philip Morris marketing practices since 1993.

"[The United Methodist] role in the campaign will increase the pressure on Philip Morris tremendously to stop hooking kids around the world with images like the Marlboro Man," says INFACT Executive Director Kathryn Mulvey.

"Philip Morris is a corporate wolf preying on the children of the world cloaked in the sheep's clothing of Kraft," said GBCS chief executive Jim Winkler. "The Kraft boycott is a constructive way to stem the tide of the global tobacco epidemic. While there has been some progress made in the US, the world's poorest and most vulnerable nations are at high risk. The tobacco industry's aggressive expansion into overseas markets has dramatically increased tobacco-related disease, death, and wreaked financial devastation due to overwhelming health care costs."

The board's decision to join nearly 200 other institutions and prominent individuals represents another liability for Philip Morris.

Despite an 800 percent increase in spending on corporate image advertising between 1998 and 1999, Philip Morris's attempts to polish its public image may be backfiring. According to a recent Harris Interactive poll, 16 percent of respondents familiar with Philip Morris had boycotted its products over the past year.

Tobacco and Alcohol Money Fund Candidates

A study by Common Cause finds that over $258 million has been spent by tobacco, gun, gambling, and alcohol interests since 1989 on US political campaigns.

All of those dollars are designed to influence legislators, and there are ways to remind them continually their voting record could determine the amount of money they or their opponents could receive in future elections.

The General Board of Church and Society says, "It is time to free Congress from this corrupting pressure through a system of public campaign financing that would take government away from special interests and return it to the people."

The agency commends those politicians of both parties who are working to achieve real campaign finance reform, and it calls upon United Methodists to work within their own states to build support for measures that would end the flood of special-interest monies to political campaigns.

What Can a Local Church Do?

- Demonstrate concern for alcohol and drug abusers and their families by supporting the care, treatment, and rehabilitation of addicts.

- Include the problems of alcohol and the value of abstinence as a part of Christian education.

- Develop prevention education for family, church, and community.

- Encourage sound empirical research on the social effects of alcohol and other legal and illegal drugs.

- Advocate campaign finance reform in order to reduce the pressure on legislators to vote with tobacco and alcohol interests.

- Oppose the sale and consumption of alcoholic beverages within the confines of church facilities.

- Discuss the problem of driving while intoxicated and impaired by alcohol or other drugs, and support legislation to reduce such activity.

- Back legislative efforts to eliminate all advertising and promoting of tobacco and alcoholic beverages.

- Urge the Federal Trade Commission to continue developing better health hazard warning statements concerning the use of alcohol.

- Join the boycott against Kraft Foods.

- Ban the use of tobacco in all church facilities.

- Support efforts to establish a tobacco-free environment in all public areas.

- Develop educational methods that discourage the use of tobacco and methods to assist those who wish to stop using tobacco.

- Urge the Department of Agriculture and other government agencies to plan for and assist the orderly economic transition of the tobacco industry—tobacco growers, processors, and distributors—into industries more compatible with the general welfare of the people.

- Work for a minimum legal drinking age of twenty-one years.

- Support strong, humane law-enforcement efforts against the illegal sale of all drugs, and urge that those arrested for possession and use of illegally procured drugs be subject to education and rehabilitation.

- Observe the annual Drug and Alcohol Awareness Sunday to challenge young people and their elders to say "no" as an aspect of their commitment to Jesus Christ.

- Promote an alternative lifestyle that encourages "wellness" without drugs and alcohol.

Teaching Plan

1. Celebrate. Prepare a pitcher of grape juice before the session begins. Invite participants to pour themselves a glass and then raise it in toast to God. Let the sentiments be lighthearted or serious. Have the group members respond to each toast with the words "To life!" or "Thanks be to God!"

2. Together, sing or read the second stanza of "Let Us Break Bread Together" *(The United Methodist Hymnal,* 618). Ask the participants to examine the texts of the Communion hymns on pages 612–41. How many of them mention wine? What message do these words convey about wine? Do you agree? Why do you think so many of them mention only the bread but not the wine?

3. Make a statement. Ask volunteers to say something about the role alcohol has played in their lives and the lives of their families and friends. From these remarks, ask the group to come up with five statements that complete the phrase: "In today's culture alcohol is. . . ."

4. Brainstorm. Imagine a local college or university has heard about the United Methodist stance on drinking and comes to you for help in developing a campaign to reduce student drinking. Brainstorm a general plan that the school might adopt. What role does religion play in your plan? How can moral suasion play a role in discouraging alcohol abuse?

5. Discuss. Alcoholism is one of the few medical conditions that is addressed with a predominantly behavioral cure. Review "The Sacred Cow" (pages 55–56) and "In All Things Moderation" (page 57). Why do you believe our society has not taken a more aggressive approach in researching a scientific or medical approach to this disease? Another legal drug—tobacco—is under attack, while alcohol still advertises with impunity. Why?

6. Divide the Core Bible Passages among the group members. Read "Debauchery" (page 54) and "Fruit of the Vine" (pages 54–55). Have participants imagine themselves as prophets. Keeping these lessons in mind, speak with the intentions of God and write three additional steps to the 12-step program of Alcoholics Anonymous. What words do you believe your "higher power" would offer to people struggling with addiction?

7. Debate. The United Methodist Church advocates complete abstinence from alcohol. Some studies have found that a single three-ounce serving of red wine daily may have medical benefits. Is this sufficient reason for the church to change its official position? Debate the following resolution: "Modern research would support that The United Methodist Church discontinue its support for total abstinence from beverage alcohol."

Discuss the willingness of persons to "consider seriously and prayerfully the witness of abstinence as part of their Christian commitment." How, specifically, might abstaining from alcohol make one a "faithful witness to God's liberating and redeeming love"? What other ways might the church or individuals begin to address the problems alcohol raises in the lives of those in the community?

8. Discuss whether a boycott of Kraft products will affect the marketing practices of Philip Morris.

9. Discuss ways in which tobacco and alcohol money can affect the voting of legislators. Would campaign financing reform help?

11. Read "The Cost" (pages 53–54). Discuss what you believe to be the most startling costs of alcohol use and abuse in our society. Ask each participant to design a monument that might be placed somewhere in the community that draws attention to the pain and suffering alcohol can bring. Include one element in the design that educates and one element that addresses answers the faith community might provide.

Chapter 6

A Pervasive Influence

Social Principle ¶162Q, "Media Violence and Christian Values"

The unprecedented impact the media (principally television and movies) are having on Christian and human values within our society becomes more apparent each day. We express disdain at current media preoccupation with dehumanizing portrayals, sensationalized through mass media "entertainment" and "news." These practices degrade humankind and violate the teachings of Christ and the Bible.

United Methodists, along with those of other faith groups, must be made aware that the mass media often undermine the truths of Christianity by promoting permissive lifestyles and detailing acts of graphic violence. Instead of encouraging, motivating, and inspiring its audiences to adopt lifestyles based on the sanctity of life, the entertainment industry often advocates the opposite, painting a cynical picture of violence, abuse, greed, profanity, and a constant denigration of the family. The media must be held accountable for the part they play in the decline of values we observe in society today. Many in the media remain aloof to the issue, claiming to reflect rather than to influence society. For the sake of our human family, Christians must work together to halt this erosion of moral and ethical values in the world community by:

1) encouraging local congregations to support and encourage parental responsibility to monitor their children's viewing and listening habits on TV, movies, radio and the Internet,

2) encouraging local congregations, parents and individuals to express their opposition to the gratuitous portrayal of violent and sexually indecent shows by writing to the stations that air them and the companies that sponsor them,

3) encouraging individuals to express their opposition to the corporate sponsors of these shows by the selection and purchase of alternate products.

Social Principle ¶162R, "The Internet"

Development of the Internet and other electronic means of communication is radically changing the way in which many people communicate. The Internet provides creative opportunities for human advancement drawing upon vast resources around the world. The positive consequences of the Internet continue to expand: adults and children can contact their peers anywhere, utilize the resources of the world to nurture their minds and spirits, and look for ways to attain their goals. Therefore, the church should promote positive uses of the Internet, and equal access to it. However, the Internet also exposes users to grave dangers. Therefore, the Internet must be managed responsibly, especially for children, in order to maximize its benefits, while minimizing the risk of exposure to inappropriate and illegal materials. Religious and civic groups should work together to make the Internet a safer place for all.

Core Bible Passages

John 17:11-15; Ephesians 5:1-20; Philippians 2:12-18

The world can be a precarious place. In most cases, life is lived as a daily routine of commonplace events and expectations. We encounter moments of high anticipation and kindness, have our times of pain and loss, and eventually succumb to decline. Our most significant questions and conflicts are seldom resolved in a few hours. That kind of life, however, does not sell. The world of the mass media demands intensity, conflict, and resolution. Life is packaged for immediate and satisfying consumption. The line between realism and unrealism is blurred to create anxiety, fascination, and desire. By doing so, the media help form a culture that is dissatisfied, probably misinformed, and bombarded with images and values that do not always accurately reflect those of family, school, and religion.

Sometimes the influence of the media can trigger dangerous emotional and psychological factors. Most psychologists are convinced that everyone learns violent behavior by seeing it enacted. The real burning of a subway tollbooth clerk duplicates a scene from an action movie. Some rapists and murderers have identified their obsessions with movie and television stars and their roles. The American Psychological Association estimates that before children have completed elementary school they will see 100,000 acts of violence on television alone.

Is It Really That Bad?

Those who defend the frequent depiction of violence in the media often point out that we live in a violent world, so why not be honest about it? Because a few may be psychologically vulnerable, why keep the rest of us from having an innocent thrill? Others have suggested that the media, like the broadcasting of the Columbine shootings or the attack on the World Trade Center force us to examine issues that we would not normally consider.

For many however, the media has created a disturbing distortion of values. Violence has been the chosen method of conflict resolution. Filmmaker Raoul Ruiz believes that American cinema has successfully convinced the world that the most appealing narrative is a clash of wills. Decisions are quickly made in these films, and problems are quickly solved (usually with force and techniques that are often not technologically reasonable). Even the most "sophisticated" police dramas on television fail to deal with the causes of social problems but respond to the dangerous extremes by brutally eliminating them. That is why the Gulf War was so easy to report, and the actions in Afghanistan so difficult. The Gulf War seemed realistic and conclusive with a "real enemy." Providing food aid and dropping bombs on Afghanistan seems far more confusing.

Extensive studies reveal a preponderance of other negative images in the media. A poll by Princeton Survey Associates found that Cubans, Mexicans, Middle Easterners, and Caribbean immigrants were often negatively depicted in the media. Women continue to be treated as subordinates or sexual objects in much of the media. Talk shows continue to focus on unusual sexual behaviors and relationships, under the guise that such open discussions can lead to healing. Soon no subject seems more important than any other. Too often meaningful dialogue is lost, and verbal exchanges deteriorate into hateful outbursts. Drugs still proliferate. The National Council on Alcoholism reports that a child will see 75,000 incidents of alcohol consumption on television before the age of 18. Tabloid news tends to dominate political or serious social coverage. Music and video games amplify the role of violence. Suggestive or overtly erotic behavior is glamourized.

Depression

Maybe the most harmful effect of violence in media is depression. Film Critic Michael Medved reported a University of Chicago survey of 25,000 eighth graders that found that immigrant children were significantly better at school than those born in the United States. The defining difference in the study seemed to be the "hopeful attitude of the immigrant parents." These parents also encouraged their children to study more and restricted their television viewing. But the longer the immigrants lived here, the more pessimistic they became. Medved is convinced that pessimism and depression are learned through the constant bombardment of media images of brutality; loveless sex; meaningless lives; and disrespect for family, religion, and cultural norms.

A United Methodist Response to Violence

We live in a climate of violence. Violence is everywhere: in city and suburb, in mean streets and quiet lanes, in New York City and Afghanistan, in private conversations and public media.

Our society knows violence through abuse and rape, rising crime rates and diminished trust. We acknowledge that the climate of the psychological violence of words as well as physical violence breeds fear and rapidly escalating concerns for personal security. This in turn leads to more violence and contributes to societies' tightening cycle of violence.

Violence is simple and brutal, but its roots are complex. We know it to be bred in families where children and spouses are abused and maltreated, where problems are met with force or threat of force. People who are in submissive positions to authority, actual or perceived, are particularly vulnerable to violence. We know that violence may be related to learning disabilities and chemical dependency. And we know that violence is exacerbated in communities and families living in poverty, and by the prominence given to it in films, television, and other media.

Women often are portrayed in the media as being subjected to sexual violation and violence. These sexual situations would appear to create no harmful effects for women, when in fact the context of the encounter is a power or authority relationship. The electronic media and film often reinforce this authority/victim relationship, depicting it as harmless or neutral.

Violence cannot be reduced to one cause. It is clear, however, that films and television play a role not only in reflecting but also in contributing to a violent and mean world.

Films and Television

■ Give the only information many receive about some aspects of life. Frequently, there are no other comparable sources of information available on human relationships or complex social issues.

■ Model and prompt emotional responses to the realities of individual and social life. Entertainment that provides a vicarious experience of violence also models a response, often one of anger and retribution.

■ Over-represent violence, with television sometimes showing as many as thirty violent acts per hour as preferred solutions to disagreements. This increases viewer concern for self-protection and a fear of going out alone. In addition, it enhances the acceptance of using violence as a solution to problems.

■ Increase an appetite and tolerance for entertainment with a violent content, since the more violence an audience sees, the more violence it will want. This appetite for violence entails an increased callousness to people who may be hurting or in need.

■ Sexualize violence by rendering it pleasurable and/or by depicting an erotic payoff for the protagonists who initiate the sexual violence.

While films and television are certainly not the only cause of a climate of violence, they bear a considerable share of the responsibility.

Our Faith Perspective

According to our biblical faith, every person we encounter is precious as one created in the image of God and one for whom Christ died (Romans 5:8-10). Every human group—all races, women and men, young and old, rich and poor, just and unjust—accordingly share in this dignity.

Our response to others is one of caring for them as we care for ourselves (Matthew 7:12). Problems are not solved through a self-protective consciousness, but through trust in God (Matthew 5:39-42). They are solved in a context of community, respect, and hearing of one another, and, where necessary, through the provisions of the broader community (Matthew 18:15-20). Any force needed to protect human life must be the minimum required and carried out in this context.

We are to be people of peace (Matthew 5:9). We are people of the story and realize the powerful impact of images. We are about what is true and honorable and just and pure (Philippians 4:8). We are accountable for our words as well as our deeds (Matthew 12:36).

We therefore deplore the competing stories of violence from the media that continue to shape our society. Even in doing so, however, we know that sin still infects and affects us all. Too often we refuse to accept our personal and corporate complicity in violence and seek to blame others for the violence in our society. Too often we are weak and uncertain about our part of the solution.

After all, we Christians:

■ Support the media industries as consumers, thereby helping to form their financial backbone. We are part of the audience that media violence attracts.

■ Permit and sometimes encourage our children's exposure to media with violent content. When a child is baptized, a congregation promises to nurture and care for the child and to bring the child into faith. We certainly must be concerned about the impact that media has on a child.

■ Participate in the media industries through our investments and through our vocations as producers and writers. We do not always use our power to work for better programming.

■ Shirk our duty as citizens to be vigilant in the pursuit of a common good.

An Issue of Urgency

Media violence has not abated. Movie rentals and cable television have made explicit violence more available. Network television has supplied a steady diet of violence; 70 percent of primetime programs depict violence, with an average of sixteen violent acts (including two murders) in each evening's primetime programming.

The American Psychological Association estimates that before children have completed elementary school they will have seen 100,000 acts of violence on television alone.

We affirm our adherence to the principles of an open forum of ideas and the guarantees of the First Amendment to free speech, press, and religion. As objectionable as we find media violence, we do not believe government censorship is a viable or appropriate solution.

We strongly object, however, to what we see as the misuse of the First Amendment, by commercial interests, as a cover for a quest for profit. Free speech and a free press have their places within a context of social responsibility and a concern for the common good. We hold media industries accountable for what they produce and distribute, and we challenge them to act as good citizens in society.

We commit ourselves to working through government and with industry to find ways to respect free expression while abhorring and selectively limiting media violence, the moral equivalent of a harmful substance. We commit ourselves also to support families and churches in their aspirations and strategies for more appropriate media choices.

Living in the Word

In John 17:11-15, Jesus, who had always cared for his disciples and prayed sincerely for their well-being, continued to care for them after his death. His petition was not simply that they be able to live in but not be of the world. It was more dramatic: that they be protected from evil while they lived in the world. One wonders if we are called to protect our young ones and ourselves from some of the harmful distortions of the media.

Ephesians 5:1-20 requires Christians to "live as children of light" who are "making the most of the time." "Obscene, silly, and vulgar talk" is entirely out of place in the Christian's life. It must be replaced with thanksgiving—a difficult thing when cynicism and pessimism often infect the media culture around us. Impure people, empty words that deceive, and darkness have no place in the kingdom of God.

Philippians 2:12-18 continues the theme of Ephesians. Christians should remain "without blemish in the midst of a crooked and perverse generation." Paul says, "Be glad and rejoice with me."

The Church in a Mass Media Culture

As proclaimers of the good news of salvation in Jesus Christ, United Methodists have traditionally been concerned about communication. Both the individualistic tradition of pietism and the communitarian tradition of the social gospel have led United Methodists to raise concerns about the distorted images and values in mass media. Therefore the denomination has agreed to

- Challenge owners and operators of mass-media institutions to be more responsible in communicating truth and more humane values;

- Advocate for access to the media and, where feasible, ownership of media institutions by marginalized groups;

- Be more responsible as a community of faith by interacting with the media and using media creatively;

- Become a model of communication by our own openness and wise use of the media; and

- Empower people to tell their own story.

However, while affirming the need for social responsibility, the denomination affirms the freedom of expression and opposes censorship. The church calls for the continual protection of the freedom of the press.

The denomination also affirms:

- The airwaves should be held in trust for the public by radio and television broadcasters and regulated in behalf of the public.

- Public broadcasting, as it continues to develop, should be supported by both public and private sectors of the society to help further the diversity of programming and information sources.

- As difficult as it may be to achieve, the goal is that all persons of every nation should have equal access to channels of communication so they can participate fully in the life of the world.

- No medium can be truly neutral. Each brings with it its own values, limitations, criteria, authoritarian or democratic structures, and selection processes.

The United Methodist Church opposes the practices of

- Emphasizing violence;

- Marketing pornography;

- Appealing to self-indulgence;

71

■ Presenting consumerism as a desired way of life;

■ Favoring the mass audience at the expense of individuals and minorities;

■ Withholding significant information;

■ Treating news as entertainment;

■ Presenting events in isolation from a larger context that would make them understandable;

■ Stereotyping characters in terms of sex roles, ethnic, or racial background, occupation, age, religion, nationality, disability, and economic status;

■ Dealing with significant political and social issues in biased and superficial ways;

■ Exhibiting an overriding concern for maximizing profit;

■ Discriminating in employment practices, particularly by failing to include women and racial or ethnic minorities in critical decision-making positions; and

■ Presenting misleading or dangerous product information or omitting essential information.

What Can a Local Church Do?

■ Provide assistance to parents of children and youth concerning how families may use television more creatively.

■ Urge the integration of media awareness and literacy programs as critical components of peace, justice, and advocacy agendas.

■ Encourage families to monitor viewing habits of television, film, and video games.

■ Discuss programs, films, and media experience in relationship to the faith.

■ Protect children from seeing films expressly intended for adults.

■ Ask US officials to review their mandated task of regulating airways. Vigilant supervision, through the Federal Communications Commission, the Federal Trade Commission, and other means, would entail a closer scrutiny of media violence than has been the case.

- Urge the media industries to contribute to the development of media standards by which we all can live. This includes the film, television, cable television, and video-games industries.

- Operate a Web page and provide information about your church and supply information to parents about ways to protect their children from pornography.

- Provide media literacy education to church members, thus equipping them to analyze and evaluate various forms of media rather than to be passive recipients.

- Empower church members to use media as a tool and to be makers of media themselves to share the gospel.

- Advocate for those shut out of the media: the poor, the less powerful, and other marginalized people.

- Recognize the close relationship between media and message; use media as channels of education, witness, evangelism, information, social services, advocacy, and ministry.

- Affirm traditional modes of face-to-face communications, such as storytelling, dialogue, songs, and indigenous cultural modes of communication.

Teaching Plan

1. List all the media that affect our lives. Ask: How much time do you allow for each medium in an average day? Compare results. Then ask: What is the most dominant form of media? What form has the least exposure? Are there any surprises in the lists?

2. Contemplate. The average child watches over 25 hours of television a week; the average adult, 27 to 42 hours. By the time teenagers graduate from high school, they will have watched about 23,000 hours of television and spent 11,000 hours in the classroom. How are youth affected by these statistics? How is the current generation of young people different from your own?

3. Discuss ways in which we can affirm freedom of speech and still protect young people from exposure to portrayals of excessive violence and sexually oriented material.

4. Read "Films and Television" (page 68). Do you agree or disagree with the following: "The showing of violence increases viewer concern for self-protection and a fear of going out alone. In addition, it enhances the acceptance of using violence as a solution to problems."

Do you agree that showing violence increases "an appetite and tolerance for entertainment with a violent content, since the more violence an audience sees, the more violence it will want"?

5. Discuss ways in which your group might be able to influence local media.

6. Read the Social Principles' statement regarding the Internet. What should your congregation do to protect young people from sexually explicit or graphic material?

Chapter 7

AIDS
Today

(Timothy Bryan and Melissa Lauber contributed to this chapter.)

Social Principle ¶162S,
"Persons Living With HIV and AIDS"

Persons diagnosed as positive for Human Immune Virus (HIV) and with Acquired Immune Deficiency Syndrome (AIDS) often face rejection from their families and friends and various communities in which they work and interact. In addition, they are often faced with a lack of adequate health care, especially toward the end of life.

All individuals living with HIV and AIDS should be treated with dignity and respect.

We affirm the responsibility of the Church to minister to and with these individuals and their families regardless of how the disease was contracted. We support their rights to employment, appropriate medical care, full participation in public education, and full participation in the Church.

We urge the Church to be actively involved in the prevention of the spread of AIDS by providing educational opportunities to the congregation and the community. The Church should be available to provide counseling to the affected individuals and their families.

Core Bible Passages

Numbers 12:1-15; Mark 1:40-45; Revelation 3:14-22

In the mountains of West Virginia they gather, people with AIDS who have assembled to rediscover hope and talk honestly with others about the disease and its effects on their lives. Sometimes there is healing. Always there is honesty.

The gatherings, sponsored by the Baltimore-Washington United Methodist Annual Conference are called Quality of Life Retreats. They bring about 30 people with AIDS and a large crew of United Methodists together for massages, variety shows, crafts, nature walks through the mountains, dancing, educational seminars on treatments and therapies, storytelling, and conversation.

The gatherings have changed over the years. The first Quality of Life Retreat began with a handful of white, gay men. But as the disease spread, the group diversified. Today there are more women and children and a different sense of living with AIDS. Yet despite the changing faces of the disease, each retreat brings startling, heart-wrenching questions.

One weekend, Agnes introduced herself to her small group. She had full-blown AIDS. She also had two small children and was pregnant. How was she going to tell her children? How could she leave them? She was even more terrified for the child that lay inside her. She did not want to bring a "motherless AIDS baby" into the world simply to die a cruel death. And yet, her faith convinced her that abortion was wrong. How could she kill her own child? "What am I supposed to do?" she asked. "What am I even supposed to think? Where is God's way in all of this?"

Leroy and Cliff were in another small group. Friends from Baltimore, they were both IV drug users and lived dangerous lives. When they were diagnosed HIV-positive within a week of one another, they went on a rampage—drinking, "doing drugs," and having unprotected sex with women. After three months, they were startled to find that they were still alive and began to face the moral consequences of their actions. They had probably passed the disease on to others, but they were too afraid to notify them.

Eventually, they joined a Narcotics Anonymous group. The Quality of Life Retreat exposed their deeper distress over their souls. In the small group they admitted that they believed in forgiveness and God's care for them. But they also believed that they were going to hell. "Can the church give us the real answers? Are we damned forever?" they asked. "If so, then what's the point?" they wondered.

In a worship service that evening, each of the participants at the retreat was wrapped in a blanket. These blankets, they were told, represented all the negative things that separated them from God and wholeness. After singing, tears, and prayer, each participant was invited to cast off his or her blanket. Many flung their blankets with abandon. Agnes let hers drop quietly. Cliff joked that he would be wearing his to his grave. Eventually, however, he dramatically spun out of it, deciding that "it might be best to choose hope."

A Global Pandemic

The number of people who have died of AIDS and who have tested HIV-positive exceeds the number of people killed during World War II.

AIDS is the fourth leading cause of death globally and one out five in Africa is dying of the virus. Of that number, 79 percent got the infection through heterosexual contact, 7 percent through homosexual contact.

Africa. Africa with only 10 percent of the world's population has 83 percent of all AIDS-related deaths worldwide. The continent reports 3.4 million new infections and 2.3 million deaths in 2001. In Swaziland, Botswana, and some areas of South Africa, more than 30 percent of pregnant women are HIV-positive. In West Africa, several countries with previously low infection numbers— including Nigeria, Africa's most populous nation—have now passed the 5 percent infection mark.

One fourth of the populations of Zimbabwe and Botswana are infected with HIV, one-fifth of the people of Namibia, Swaziland, and Zambia. South Africa's infection rate is 14 percent and growing rapidly.

About half of the new HIV infections worldwide are in young people 15 to 24.

Eastern Europe. The Joint United Nations Programme on HIV/AIDS (UNAIDS) reports that the number of HIV infections in Eastern Europe is rising faster than anywhere else in the world. Reported figures are largely underestimated but even so, the latest figures reveal there were more than 75,000 reported new infections in Russia by November 2001, a 15-fold increase in just three years.

"HIV is spreading rapidly throughout the entire Eastern European region—a quarter of a million new cases only this year," said Dr. Peter Piot, executive director of the UNAIDS. "HIV/AIDS is unequivocally the most devastating disease we have ever faced, and it will get worse before it gets better."

"Low reported national prevalence rates can be misleading," said Dr. Gro Harlem Brundtland, director-general of the World Health Organization, "because they may be exceedingly high in certain sub-populations. In many countries, we have to take these figures as warning signs of an impending epidemic, not as excuses for complacency." In countries with high populations, a few percentage points can translate into millions of infected individuals.

Asia. In Asia, figures also continue to climb and for the first time. Despite effective prevention efforts in some smaller countries, the number of newly infected people reached one million. In some Middle Eastern countries as yet virtually untouched by HIV, infection is beginning to spread rapidly among high-risk groups.

Calls for Action

United Methodist Bishop Nkulu Ntanda Ntambo of Zambia recently told his fellow bishops that the time for being "philosophical" about AIDS is over. "We need your action, the action of your churches and your governments. People are dying," he declared. He said the discussion of sex is taboo in his culture. "It is killing millions of people, but nobody is allowed to talk about it."

United Methodist Bishop Fritz Mutti, leader of the church's Kansas Area, and his wife Etta Mae, lost two sons to AIDS. They recently told a story of a hospital in India straining to serve an increasing number of AIDS patients and of the reluctance of Christians to get involved. "If AIDS was caused by the bite of a mosquito, the Christian community would be at the forefront of providing care," the bishop said.

The Reverend Fred Smith, a United Methodist pastor and seminary professor from Pittsburgh, reports that one in 50 black men and one in 160 black women in the United States are HIV-positive, "and yet we don't believe we have a problem."

United Methodist Bishop Joseph Sprague, leader of the church's Chicago area, says the AIDS crisis and poverty must be dealt with through reflection, research, and action. "We United Methodists are experts in reflection and research, but now it is time to act," he said.

Disease and Compassion

In Numbers 12:1-15, Miriam and Aaron criticized Moses for marrying a Cushite woman (Zipporah). They claimed that God also speaks through them and not only through Moses. For this action, God struck Miriam with a skin disease. For no apparent reason, Aaron was not punished at all. She languished in exile for seven days because of her disease.

That Miriam alone was punished strikes us as unfair, arbitrary, and sexist. As in the story of Job where God allows Satan to inflict Job with sores, disease was sometimes understood by the ancient Hebrews as having a divine cause. They knew nothing of germs or the science of epidemics, and cures; and so these stories reflect ancient attempts to come to some understanding about how arbitrary disease can be.

How strikingly different is the theological picture we have in Jesus and the early church. Jesus encountered a disease-stricken exile while traveling in Galilee (Mark 1:40-45) He did not claim God's judgment on the man's leprosy, but was filled with compassion and drew the man back into society by being willing to touch and to heal him.

Terrible epidemics in the Roman Empire in the second and third century are believed to have killed up to a third of the population. While many pagans ran from the cities leaving their families to die, Christians became famous for their compassion for the sick. Their care for the sick and dying was a powerful witness.

For Jesus and for those who follow him, disease is a cause for compassion, not for moral judgment.

What Can One Person Do?

Anne Garwood and Ben Melnick in *What Everyone Can Do to Fight AIDS* (Jossey Bass, 1995) offers some suggestions:

- Get to know people with AIDS.

- Read books or watch movies about AIDS.

- Volunteer for an AIDS service organization in your community.

- Don't misspeak about AIDS, especially using the words *victim*, which implies powerlessness, or *innocent victim*, which suggests a moral judgment. Instead use the term *persons living with AIDS*.

- Don't ask persons who are HIV-positive how they became infected.

- Be yourself.

- Don't be afraid to touch them.

- Don't treat them with pity.

- When providing food for persons with AIDS, be aware of their special health needs. Wash fruits and vegetables, do not undercook foods, avoid dairy products, and have decaffeinated beverages available. Use precaution if you have a cold or flu.

Teaching Plan

1. First Impressions. Give each participant a piece of paper and a pencil. Have them write the first thing that they think of when they hear the word *AIDS*. Let every participant read his or her first impressions to the rest of the group. Discuss: Did your initial response disturb you? Did any of the responses encourage or show hope? What responses seemed to occur most often? How do these responses affect our approach to AIDS?

2. Read the beginning story (pages 75–76). Ask: What moral and ethical issues are raised? How do you respond to Agnes when she asks where God is in her dilemma? How do you respond to Cliff and Leroy? What is the point of faith for Cliff and Leroy? Does the gospel demand we take any responsibility for the pain and suffering we cause others? What do you think about the exercise of "unwrapping" oneself from the blanket? What is the nature of God's forgiveness? of our forgiveness?

3. Read "A Global Pandemic" (pages 77–78). Ask: What information in these sections surprised you? In your opinion, what can be done to address the global AIDS crisis? Using a chalkboard or piece of posterboard, generate ideas in your group about possible responses. Which ones are responses the church could make? the federal government? other organizations?

4. Read "What Can One Person Do? (page 79). Ask the group to consider each of the recommendations. Discuss why they are important in ministry. Ask: Would any suggestions on the list be difficult for you? If so, why? What personal experiences do you have that testify to the importance of these practices and principles.

5. Review the actions taken by Glide Church in San Francisco and Vestavia Church in Birmingham. (See "Local Action Reports" that follow.) Ask: How is the community surrounding your church responding to AIDS/HIV? Does the action of other United Methodist congregations suggest some strategies for ministry your congregation might undertake?

6. Sing the hymn, "Jesus' Hands Were Kind Hands" *(The United Methodist Hymnal*, 273). Pray together the prayer, "For the Spirit of Truth" *(Hymnal*, 597).

Local Action Reports

Vestavia Hills United Methodist Church in Birmingham, Alabama, began an AIDS-care team in 1992 when Joe Elmore was pastor. The team ministered to several persons before they died and has ministered to two persons with AIDS for the last four years.

A second team was formed in 1996 to help a maternal grandmother care for two children whose parents had died of AIDS. Called the "Tanya Team" after the mother, the group helped the children purchase school clothes and supplies. Team members tutored the children, and in January 2002, the group helped the family negotiate a lease/purchase arrangement for a new home.

In addition to these two teams, a "Matthew 25:35 Team" delivers food to persons living with AIDS and a fourth team provides meals for a support group at "Birmingham AIDS Outreach," an interdenominational team providing care for persons living with AIDS.

A "Cherish the Children" team relates to an HIV treatment clinic at a children's hospital. That group provides baskets of 18 to 20 items needed by infants born to mothers who are patients at the clinic. Church members also operate a clothes closet for these families.

Glide Memorial United Methodist Church in San Francisco provides a health clinic to individuals. They offer free and confidential HIV screening and testing on every third Sunday and every Monday through Thursday. Over the course of 2001–2002, Glide's HIV Counseling, Testing, and Referral program conducted 1,238 HIV tests to residents in the surrounding areas. The outreach team reached 12,000 individuals, distributing 10,000 condom kits, 8,000 hygiene kits, 3,000 bleach kits, and provided education and referrals to promote risk reduction.

Glide Memorial is the only service provider in San Francisco that has been selected to be a Rapid HIV Testing Site, a two-year pilot project. Rapid testing, when combined with Glide's client-centered health services, case management, and counseling programs, will be a powerful tool in reducing HIV in San Francisco and promoting a holistic approach to individual care and community health.

Chapter 8

Correcting Injustices in Health Care

Social Principle ¶162T, "Right to Health Care"

Health is a condition of physical, mental, social, and spiritual well-being, and we view it as a responsibility—public and private. Health care is a basic human right. Psalm 146 speaks of the God "who executes justice for the oppressed; / who gives food to the hungry. / The Lord sets the prisoners free; / the Lord opens the eyes of the blind." It is unjust to construct or perpetuate barriers to physical wholeness or full participation in community.

We encourage individuals to pursue a healthy lifestyle and affirm the importance of preventative health care, health education, environmental and occupational safety, good nutrition, and secure housing in achieving health. We also recognize the role of governments in ensuring that each individual has access to those elements necessary to good health.

Core Bible Passage

Matthew 9:20-22

We all recognize the need for adequate health care for our families and ourselves. In the last two decades there have been many options brought before the people of this nation and some have been serious attempts to provide health care for all. However, most proposals have continued to exclude some portion of society from access to adequate health care. The debates seem to have subsided, but problems of providing adequate care to individuals are actually increasing with time.

Large Medicaid budget cuts are pending. These cuts would surely further limit health-care access for the poor and the physically or mentally challenged. Another issue is the role of Health Maintenance Organizations (HMOs) and the like. These organizations often employ persons with little or no medical training to make treatment decisions. Many insurance companies hire nurses to review the physicians' diagnoses and treatment plans. While it is unusual for nurses to oversee physicians, it is also evident that these nurses have had no contact with the patient under review.

Decisions are made with primary consideration for the costs to the corporation, not for the optimal health of the patient. In the current climate, physicians who prescribe treatments or tests not pre-approved by the insurance corporation face severe financial penalties or other disincentives to providing optimal patient care.

There is evidence that some HMOs have denied legitimate claims by requiring prior approval before treatment. It has been estimated that today's physician spends about one-third of his or her time satisfying these regulations and seeking approvals for treatment, time the physician could be spending with patients. Because there are so many public and private health-care insurance organizations, the result is an insurmountable bureaucratic maze. It is a system that tends to confuse virtually every aspect of insurance coverage for the patients and the practitioners.

Managed Care was supposed to be a way of providing care to increasing numbers of patients; however, it has actually increased the number of uninsured. The very poor, the affluent, the employees of government and large corporations, and many receiving adequate pensions plus Medicare are insured. The self-employed, recently unemployed, middle income, and working poor simply cannot afford personal health-care insurance policies. Even though some states are developing programs to provide health care to all minors regardless of family income, once the child reaches the age of majority he or she joins the ranks of the uninsured. The approval process is difficult for patients to understand, and physicians find it difficult to be in compliance with complex rules.

Various levels of government try to fill the gaps that exist in the Medicaid systems. While Medicaid (some states have different names for similar programs) provides some care to the poor, it does not encourage primary or comprehensive care and disqualifies applicants with borderline incomes. Also, the Medicaid systems remain under constant attack as one of the first places to cut state budgets. Politicians may claim health care is a priority, but actual funding is the clearest indicator of public policy priorities.

Since it is unconscionable for any human being to be denied access to adequate health care due to economic, racial, or class barriers, The United Methodist Church calls for a comprehensive single-payer program that will provide adequate health care to all without placing further barricades to access. The denomination believes health care is a basic human right and is an entitlement for all United States citizens, including Native Americans and legal resident aliens.

Contributing Factors to Poor Health

Environmental Factors. Clean air, pure water, effective sanitary systems for the disposal of wastes, nutritious foods, adequate housing, and hazard-free workplaces are essential to health. The best medical system cannot preserve or maintain health when the environment is disease-producing.

Social Factors. Inadequate education, poverty, unemployment, lack of access to food, stress-producing conditions, and social pressures reinforced by marketing and advertising strategies that encourage the use of guns, tobacco, alcohol, and other drugs are detrimental to good health.

Personal Habits. Overeating or eating non-nutritious foods, substance abuse (including alcohol, tobacco, barbiturates, sedatives, and so forth) are clearly destructive to health. Failure to exercise or to rest and relax adequately are also injurious to health. Overeating and undereating, due to food security emergencies or eating disorders, are opposite but not unrelated health crises.

What Can a Local Church Do?

- Make health concerns a priority in the church. Have special emphases that include but are not limited to women's health concerns; appropriate, unbiased, informed diagnosis and treatment of older adults; preventive care (including health education); special health concerns and needs of children and youth; and establishment of networks for information sharing and action suggestions.

- Accept responsibility for educating and motivating members to follow a healthy lifestyle reflecting our affirmation of life as God's gift.

- Become actively involved at all levels in the development of support systems for health care in the community, including dependent care (respite and 24-hour care, in-home and short-term out-of-home care), meals-on-wheels, hospice, programs for women in crisis, halfway houses, support systems for independent living, and family-support systems.

- Advocate for a healthful environment; accessible, affordable health care; continued public support for the health care of persons unable to provide for themselves; continued support for health-related research; and provision of church facilities to enable health-related ministries.

■ Search for Christian understanding of health, healing, and wholeness and the dimensions of spiritual healing in our congregations and seminaries.

■ Support public policies and programs that will ensure comprehensive health-care services of high quality to all persons on the principle of equal access.

■ Select a Sunday to celebrate as Health Care Sabbath. Use it as a time for thanksgiving for the health and well-being enjoyed by many in our world community and thanksgiving for the diverse caregivers who minister to our needs. Pray for those who are sick, who struggle with chronic illnesses, who lack access to the health-care services they need.

■ Sponsor a parish nurse to provide health-care examinations and referral information.

Teaching Plan

1. Read Matthew 9:20-22. Jesus told the woman who touched his cloak that her faith had healed her. Ask: Do you know of situations where faith has healed someone? Is there a difference between faith and positive attitudes?

2. Talk about HMOs. Ask members to talk about experiences with Health Maintenance Organizations (HMOs). Ask: Were you able to receive the health care you needed?

3. Poor or good health? Ask: What environmental factors in your community might contribute to poor or good health? What social factors exist that might contribute to poor or good health? What personal habits do members have that might contribute to poor or good health?

4. Take an inventory of your church's facilities for persons with handicapping conditions. Should any changes be made? If so, what and why? How does your church provide for persons with Parkinson's disease, autism, or other health problems?

Local Action Reports

Centenary United Methodist Church in downtown Richmond, Virginia, joined with Cross-Over Health Center to form a walk-in clinic.

The clinic provides medical, dental, and vision services for uninsured, working poor and homeless people. Five area United Methodist churches provide lunch at the Friday midday clinic, which is held in conjunction with a worship service.

A physician, nurse, and medical assistant staff the clinic. They provide medical and nursing care, medications, screenings, immunizations, health education, preventive care, and referrals to other community services. More than 1,000 patients visited the clinic in the first two years of operation.

Tarrytown United Methodist Church, a suburban community north of New York City, offers a worship service for autistic children. The pastor, the Reverend Lynne Severance, said autistic children perceive things in fragments and are often unable to follow anything sequential. Cut off from the world, they compensate by creating a mysterious world of their own. Yet, Severance said, "children and adults with autism hold within them the same longings [as all people] to seek and know God.

"I see the children who come to family church respond to that longing," the pastor said. "One boy watches the sunlight shining through the stained-glass windows. Another bounces out of his seat to dance and spin with me the moment the organ plays the first chord of the closing hymn."

Chapter 9

Christian-Muslim Relationships

(John Peterson and Paul Stroble contributed to this chapter.)

Social Principle ¶162B,
"Rights of Religious Minorities"

Religious persecution has been common in the history of civilization. We urge policies and practices that ensure the right of every religious group to exercise its faith free from legal, political, or economic restrictions. We condemn all overt and covert forms of religious intolerance, being especially sensitive to their expression in media stereotyping. We assert the right of all religions and their adherents to freedom from legal, economic, and social discrimination.

Core Bible Passages

Genesis 12:1-3; 16:1-16; 21:1-7; 21:8-21; 25:7-18

One fifth of the world's population—1.2 billion people—are Muslim, 85 percent non-Arabs. By the end of the twenty-first century, one quarter of the world's population is expected to be Muslim. Indonesia—a country halfway around the world from the Middle East—is the world's largest Muslim nation. Islam has also made marked inroads in the West. Excluding Turkey, there are 20 million Muslims living in Europe.

Even the United States, often perceived as a bastion of Judeo-Christian culture, is experiencing a rapid increase in its Muslim population. An estimated seven million Muslims live in the United States, an increase of one million since 1995. If the current rate of growth holds steady, experts predict Islam will soon surpass Judaism as the second largest religion in this nation. With more than 1,200 mosques sprinkled across the country—a 25 percent increase over the past six years—people in the United States can no longer assume their neighbors share their faith.

Increasing religious diversity is testing our tolerance and forcing us to evaluate our commitment to pluralism.

Backlash

Unfortunately, the growing visibility of Muslims in the United States has not resulted in a commensurate increase in understanding. Instead, the violent actions of a few extremists have distorted the image of Islam and our Muslim neighbors. In 1998, half the respondents to a Roper Poll described Islam as anti-American, anti-Western, or supportive of terrorism.

This misconception once resulted in reports of discrimination; but after the September 11, 2001, terrorist violence, friction turned to open hostility. In the week following the World Trade Center tragedy, the Council on American-Islamic Relations (CAIR) recorded an anti-Muslim backlash consisting of hundreds of incidents of harassment, intimidation, violence, and even murder. The abuse has put Muslims on edge.

"Muslims have received many messages of support from people of other faiths," says CAIR executive director Nihad Awad. "Unfortunately, the bigoted acts of a small minority are creating an atmosphere of apprehension and fear in the American-Muslim community."

Salaam

The misguided anger directed toward Muslims is the consequence of ignorance. To begin with, many in the United States are unaware that Islam, which means "submission," is a religion of peace. In fact, the word *Islam* is derived from the Arabic word for "peace," *salaam.* Founded 14 centuries ago by the prophet Muhammad, Islam worships the same God (Allah) that called Abraham out of Ur.

Fiercely monotheistic, Islam rejects the Trinitarian claims of Christianity. Yet it reveres Abraham, Moses, and Jesus as prophets, albeit lesser than Muhammad. Muslims claim God gave Muhammad a final revelation—the Qur'an. "If Christ is the Word of God made flesh," says author Toby Lester, then "the [Qur'an] is the Word of God made text."

The task of the Muslim is to live out the code of conduct revealed in the Qur'an.

There are Five Pillars or Foundations of Practice:

(1) Shahada—the testimony that there is no God but Allah and Muhammad is his messenger;

(2) Salat—the recitation of five daily prayers while facing Mecca;

(3) Zakat—charity to the needy;

(4) Fasting—the month-long fast during Ramadan that fosters spiritual discipline, community, and compassion for the hungry; and

(5) Hajj—the pilgrimage to Mecca that each Muslim is expected to undertake at least once during his or her lifetime, if possible.

Following the Five Pillars, Islam developed a historical reputation as a tolerant faith that dealt justly with religious minorities under its sway.

Muhammad and his followers also earned the respect of the Western world through their military exploits; however, the Qur'an places strict limitations on the employment of violence. Neither forced conversion nor the slaughter of innocent civilians is allowed.

The Qur'an says, "Show [civilians] kindness and deal with them justly" (chapter 60, verse 8). Elsewhere the prophet Muhammad is quoted as saying: "Neither kill the old . . . nor children and babes nor the females." Even the killing of enemy soldiers is forbidden if war has not been declared. "It's basically the Geneva Convention," says Jamal Badawi, a respected Islamic interpreter.

The American-Muslim Community

A second reason the U.S. may fear Islam is lingering memories of a militant Black Muslim sect. During the 1960s, the Nation of Islam preached a doctrine of racial hatred. God was black, and whites were blue-eyed devils. When its leader Elijah Muhammad, died in 1975, his son and successor, Warith Deen Muhammad, denounced many of his father's views. He led the Black Muslim movement into the mainstream Sunni Islam and encouraged U.S. Muslims of different races to worship together.

"I've become almost a fanatical supporter of the United States government," he said in 1998. "To me, the vision of the Founding Fathers is the vision that we have in Islam."

Today, a majority of the Muslim community in the United States shares his enthusiasm. Demographically, immigrants taking full advantage of the opportunities the United States has to offer have swelled their numbers. Many are highly educated professionals—52 percent have earned graduate degrees—and are compensated accordingly.

In an article published in 2000 in *Commentary* magazine, conservative author Daniel Pipes, writes, "In socioeconomic terms . . . Muslims can find little fault with America. . . . Immigrant Muslims tend to concentrate in the professions (especially medicine and engineering) or in entreprenuership, and their income appears to be higher than the United States national average. This year, median household income was said to be $69,000."

Politically, Muslims are also taking their place within the United States mainstream. Socially conservative, they tend to vote for "family values." In the 2000 presidential race, 70 percent of the Muslim community voted for George W. Bush. They are pro-gun control, pro-environment, and supportive of the death penalty. They are vehemently anti-terrorist.

Referring to the terrorists who carried out the violence on September 11, 2001, Sheik Tah Jabir Alalwani, president of the Graduate School of Islamic and Social Studies, spoke for the entire Muslim community when he said, "If they claim they are Muslim, I would say they are not."

The Challenges Ahead

Life in the United States presents challenges to the adherents of Islam. Muslims are attempting to adapt to a society that they generally find highly permissive. Like many Christians, they are offended by the immorality of popular culture.

Muslim immigrants argue with an increasingly Americanized second generation over the use of alcohol, dating, and eating pork, all of which are forbidden in Islam. They are self-conscious about the stares they receive when they prostate themselves in prayer, wear their head scarves (hijabs), or ask for time off to attend worship on Friday afternoons.

Christians have played a crucial role in easing their transition by promoting a culture of peace and understanding. By reaching out to our Muslim neighbors, we become agents of reconciliation and healing. Jesus Christ calls us to be peacemakers, and certainly there has never been a greater need for peace than now.

Father Abraham

The world's three great monotheistic faiths—Judaism, Christianity, and Islam—trace their roots back to Abraham, whose story unfolds in Genesis.

Called by God, Abraham sets off for an unknown land, finally settling in Hebron (13:18). Unable to bear children, his wife Sarah offered her Egyptian maidservant, Hagar, as a surrogate mother, a common practice in ancient times (30:1-3).

However, jealousy crept into the arrangement. Upon conceiving, Hagar became contemptuous of Sarah's infertility. Enraged, Sarah drove Hagar into the desert where she met the angel of the Lord. Convincing her to return, the angel promised Hagar a son, who was to be named Ishmael because God had heard her affliction; and he would have descendents beyond count (16:10).

Hagar's troubles were not over. When Sarah delivered Isaac, Hagar and Ishmael were expelled. God heard Ishmael's cries and provided water in the wilderness, promising Hagar a second time to "make a great nation out of [Ishmael]" (21:18). While Judaism traces its lineage back to Isaac, Islam claims this promise and reveres Ishmael as the prophet Mohammed's progenitor.

The Qur'an says: "Ibrahim was neither Jew nor a Christian." The biblical text lacks such religious rivalry. Instead, Isaac and Ishmael burried their father together (25:7-18). As evidenced by the biblical genealogy that follows, God kept faith with both of Abraham's sons and blessed them.

Areas of Conflict

Islam is a growing religion, one that proclaims peace. Sometimes it comes into conflict with other religions of the world, and Christianity is no exception. For example, Saudi Arabia "still has the world's worst record of persecuting Christians," according to Brother Andrew of *Open Doors*.

Brother Andrew, who has tracked religious persecution for 40 years, says that in Saudi Arabia five children were arrested January 7, 2000, at a worship service in Riyadh, along with ten adults. Some feared the Saudi interrogators might force children to reveal details about their parents' involvement in Christian fellowship meetings.

In the Sudan, two million people, mostly African Christians, have died. According to the Center for Religious Freedom, the Sudanese government and its agents are "enslaving and raping thousands of women and children . . . and forcibly converting Christian boys." Further, they report that individual Christians, "including clergy," have frequently been imprisoned, flogged, tortured, and assassinated for their faith.

Perhaps the most publicized event of religious persecution was when the ruling Taliban government in Afghanistan held eight members of the Shelter Now International assistance group. The group was freed by the Northern Alliance and brought out of that nation by US military personnel.

Teaching Plan

1. Pray together "Praising God of Many Names" (*The United Methodist Hymnal*, 104).

2. Ask these questions and discuss: What is the first word that comes to mind when you say the word *Muslim*? Ask: How do we stereotype Muslims? What role do the media and popular culture play in our understanding of our Muslim neighbors?

Understanding the Judeo-Christian culture as the "west" and Islam as the "east," what are the issues that currently hinder "one great fellowship of love"? What are things that divide the two traditions? What things do they have in common?

3. Read "Areas of Conflict" (pages 92–93). Every culture has its extremist element or elements (think of David Koresh or Marshall Applewhite. Ask: How do these stories of extremist Muslims affect your feelings toward all Muslims? Why is it so hard for some people to separate extremists from moderates?

4. Read the Core Bible Passages and "Father Abraham" (pages 91–92). Ask participants to tell the story of Abraham in their own words. Consider the events from the viewpoints of the various characters: Abraham, Sarah, Hagar, Ishmael, and Isaac. Ask: Why do Muslims revere Abraham? Ishmael? Why is it significant that Judaism, Christianity, and Islam trace their lineage to Abraham? Is it important that Ishmael and Isaac buried their father together? Why or why not?

5. Consider: Islam is growing so rapidly in the United States that it will soon replace Judaism as the country's second largest religion. Does Islam's success challenge Christianity?

Does the United States need to make accomodations to Islam? If so, what? What role can the church play in welcoming Muslims?

6. Close with singing "Source and Sovereign, Rock and Cloud" (*Hymnal*, 113).

Alternative Teaching Plan

It is possible in many communities to invite a guest from an Islamic community to meet with a church group. Alternatively, by prior arrangement, most Muslims will welcome groups to observe one of their prayer services. It might be helpful if the visiting group would prepare questions in advance and provide those questions to the host group prior to the visit. The women in the group should ask in advance what is considered acceptable attire in an Islamic center. Certain forms of dress are considered offensive.

Local Action Report

On November 30, 2001, a group of 50 United Methodists in Indiana, including Indiana Area bishop Woodie White, visited the Center of Islam in the United States. The Center is located near Plainfield, Indiana, southeast of Indianapolis. "The Methodist Church has shown leadership in America in understanding Islam," Dr. Sayyid Syeed, director of the Islamic Society of North America, told the group. He referred specifically to a brochure published by the General Board of Global Ministries, *Our Muslim Neighbors*. The group went to the center's mosque to worship, meet with staff, and learn more about Islam.

Chapter 10

Christian-Jewish Dialogue

Social Principle ¶162B, "Rights of Religious Minorities"

Religious persecution has been common in the history of civilization. We urge policies and practices that ensure the right of every religious group to exercise its faith free from legal, political, or economic restrictions. We condemn all overt and covert forms of religious intolerance, being especially sensitive to their expression in media stereotyping. We assert the right of all religions and their adherents to freedom from legal, economic, and social discrimination.

Core Bible Passage

1 Corinthians 1:18–31

What kind of relationship can Christians have with the Jewish community? That's the question The United Methodist Church has been addressing for the past three decades. A major step in our understanding of Christian-Jewish relations was taken in 1972, when General Conference adopted a position statement under the title Bridge in Hope. This denominational statement urged church members and congregations to undertake "serious new conversations" with Jews in order to promote "growth in mutual understanding."

Especially crucial for Christians in our quest for understanding has been the struggle to recognize the Holocaust as the catastrophic culmination of a long history of anti-Jewish attitudes and actions in which individual Christians, and sometimes the church itself, have been deeply implicated. Dialogue with Jewish partners has been central for Christians in the process of learning about the scope of the Holocaust atrocities; acknowledgment of Christian complicity; and responsibility, repentance, and commitment to work against anti-Semitism in all its forms in the future.

The Basis for Dialogue

There is one living God, in whom both Jews and Christians believe.

While the Jewish and Christian traditions understand and express their faith in the same God in significantly different ways, Christians believe with Paul that God, who was in Christ reconciling the world to God's own self (2 Corinthians 5:18-19), is none other than the maker of heaven and earth whom both Jews and Christians worship. Above all else, Christians and Jews are bonded in joyful and faithful response to the one God, with each community living out its unique response to God's call.

Jesus was a devout Jew as were his first followers. We know that understanding our Christian faith begins by recognizing and appreciating this seminal fact. Neither the ministry of Jesus and his apostles nor the worship and thought of the early church can be understood apart from the Jewish tradition, culture, and worship of the first century. Further, we believe that God's revelation in Jesus Christ is unintelligible apart from the story of what God did in the life of the people of Israel.

Because Christianity has deep Jewish roots, it is understood that knowledge of our origins is essential to our faith. As expressed in a statement from the Consultation on the Church and Jewish People of the World Council of Churches: "We give thanks to God for the spiritual treasure we share with the Jewish people: faith in the living God of Abraham, Isaac, and Jacob; knowledge of the name of God and of the commandments; the prophetic proclamation of judgment and grace; the Hebrew Scriptures; and the hope of the coming Kingdom. In all these, we find common roots in biblical revelation and see spiritual ties that bind us to the Jewish people." Judaism and Christianity are living and dynamic religious movements that have continued to evolve since the time of Jesus, often in interaction with each other and with God's continual self-disclosure in the world.

Christians often have little understanding of the history of Judaism as it has developed since the lifetime of Jesus. As a World Council of Churches publication points out: "Bible-reading and worshiping Christians often believe that they 'know Judaism' since they have the Old Testament, the records of Jesus' debates with Jewish teachers, and the early Christian reflections on the Judaism of their times. . . . This attitude is often reinforced by lack of knowledge about the history of Jewish life and thought through the 1,900 years since the parting of the ways of Judaism and Christianity."

Judaism Continues to Develop New Traditions

As Christians, it is important for us to recognize that the Jewish community developed vital new traditions of its own after the time of Jesus. After the loss of the Temple in A.D. 70, Rabbinic Judaism emerged and continues as a vital, vibrant tradition that shapes Jewish religious and cultural life. This evolving tradition has given the Jewish people profound spiritual resources for creative life through the centuries. We increase our understanding when we learn about the rich variety of contemporary Jewish faith practice, theological interpretation, and worship.

We believe that Christians and Jews are bound to God though biblical covenants that are eternally valid. We believe that Jesus was sent by God to redeem all people, and that in Christ the biblical covenant has been made radically new. However, we do not believe that earlier covenant relationships have been invalidated or that God has abandoned the covenant with the Hebrew people.

We believe that just as God is steadfastly faithful to the biblical covenant in Jesus Christ, God is likewise steadfastly faithful to the biblical covenant with the Jewish people. The covenant God established with the Jewish people through Abraham, Jacob, and Moses continues because it is an eternal covenant. Paul proclaims that the gift and call of God to the Jews is irrevocable (Romans 11:29). Thus, we believe that the Jewish people continue in covenant relationship with God.

Misuse of Scripture

Historical and contemporary misuse of Scripture has fostered negative attitudes toward and actions against Jews. Use of New Testament passages that blame "the Jews" for the crucifixion of Jesus have throughout history been the basis of many acts of discrimination against Jews, frequently involving physical violence. There is no doubt that traditional and often officially sanctioned and promulgated Christian teachings, including the uncritical use of anti-Jewish New Testament writings, have caused untold misery and form the basis of modern anti-Semitism.

It is essential for Christians to oppose forcefully anti-Jewish acts and rhetoric that persist in the present time in many places. We must be zealous in challenging overt and subtle anti-Semitic stereotypes and bigoted attitudes that ultimately made the Holocaust possible. These lingering patterns are a call to Christians for ever-new educational efforts and continued vigilance, so that we, remembering and honoring the cries of the tortured and the dead, can claim with Jews around the world to be faithful to the post-Holocaust cry of "never again."

Should Christians Proclaim Christ to Jews?

As Christians we are called to proclaim the good news of Jesus Christ to all people. Yet, we also understand that the issues of the evangelization of persons of other faiths, and of Jews in particular, are sensitive and difficult. While Christians respond to the call to proclaim the gospel, we also know that we can never understand fully the extent of God's work in the world. We recognize that God can also work outside the Christian church. We know that any judgment about who is ultimately saved belongs only to God.

The best way to relate to persons of other faith communities is through dialogue. Rather than a one-sided address or a series of monologues, dialogue combines offering an explanation of one's faith with listening. It is the intentional engagement with persons who hold other faith perspectives for purposes of mutual understanding, cooperation, and transformation.

Dialogue may be as informal as a conversation in the marketplace or as formal as the leader of one religious group explaining to others its belief or worship life. Dialogue is more than an individual or academic enterprise. It involves groups or communities of people holding different convictions who reach out to one another. This community orientation gives a practical bent to interreligious dialogue.

Through dialogue with persons of other faith communities, new insights are received regarding God's activity in the world today, the divine purpose for humankind as a whole, and the place of the Christian community within these purposes. Through dialogue, Christians find their own beliefs clarified and strengthened. We trust in the Holy Spirit to make known new and different insights through such encounters.

The only precondition for dialogue—sometimes a challenging one—is a true willingness to enter a relationship of mutual acceptance, openness, and respect. Effective dialogue requires that both partners have deep convictions about life, faith, and salvation. True dialogue does not require Christians to suspend their fundamental convictions concerning the truth of the gospel. Effective dialogue requires Christians be open to persons of other faith communities, to their convictions about life, truth, and salvation, and to their witness. Dialogue is a form of Christian ministry, not because it seeks to convert or change others but because it deepens our own faith.

Dialogue at its most profound level is an exchange of witness. Participants share with each other their perceptions of the meaning of life, of ultimate reality, salvation and hope, and the resources of their faith for enabling community. In genuine dialogue, we witness and are witnessed to. The most effective dialogue takes place when both sides really do care that the other hear, understand, and receive the other's wisdom. Part of our witness is our openness to hearing the witness of the other.

What Can a Local Church Do?

- Identify the various faith communities in your area and begin to familiarize your congregation with them. This may involve planned experiences that bring faith communities into contact with one another or the formation of study groups that provide an introduction to other faith traditions.

- Initiate dialogues with other faith communities, remaining sensitive to areas of historic tension yet open to the possibilities for deepened understanding and new insight. Each partner must forthrightly face the issues that cause separation as well as those that create unity.

- Work in practical ways with persons of other faith communities to resolve economic, social, cultural, and political problems in the community. Soup kitchens, food pantries, Habitat for Humanity projects, and other such efforts can be an effective focus for shared concerns for the common good.

- Together with persons of other faith traditions, plan community celebrations with an interreligious perspective. Prepare carefully. Sensitivity to the integrity of each tradition is essential. Care should be taken not to relativize all religious symbols and practices nor minimize religious differences.

- Develop new models of community-building that strengthen relationships and allow people to dwell together in harmony while honoring the integrity of their differences.

- As a sign of our contrition and our solidarity with the Jewish community, observe Yom HaShoah, Holocaust Memorial Day, each spring.

Teaching Plan

1. Read 1 Corinthians 1:18-31. Paul told members of the church at Corinth that Jews demanded "signs" and that they viewed a crucified Christ as a "stumbling block." For what signs were members of the Jewish community looking at the time of Jesus? What signs do they seek today? Why is a crucified Christ a "stumbling block"?

2. Discuss: How has the Holocaust changed the world's view of Jews today? Does it affect the way in which you view Jews today?

3. Ask: Has anyone visited the Holocaust Museum in Washington, D.C.? If so, ask the person(s) to share information about the experience. Has anyone visited one of the concentration camps in Germany? Share this experience as well.

What signs of prejudice against Jews linger in your community?

4. Roleplay. Ask two class members to roleplay a Christian who tells a Jewish friend that he or she is going to suffer eternal damnation if he or she doesn't convert to Christianity. Ask two other members to roleplay a Christian and a Jew who share information about their faith with one another. Discuss the differences.

Local Action Report

In 1999, the California-Nevada Annual Conference of The United Methodist Church interrupted its meeting to leap to the aid of three Sacramento synagogues that were struck by arson. Their action led the city's Jewish community to heartfelt tears of appreciation.

The predawn arson attack destroyed the extensive library and damaged the sanctuary of the oldest synagogue west of the Mississippi and caused damage to two other local synagogues.

Hate literature left at the crime scene identified the perpetrators as "Slavs" who said they "would never allow the international Jew World Order to take our land." The flier featured a cartoon of bombs raining on President Clinton and Secretary of State Madeleine Albright.

More than 1,200 United Methodists, in Sacramento, California, for their annual meeting, passed a resolution supporting the Jewish community and condemning the action. The assembly contributed $6,200 to the synagogues.